BRITISH TROLLEYBUS SYSTEMS
LONDON AND SOUTH-EAST ENGLAND

AN HISTORIC OVERVIEW

BRITISH TROLLEYBUS SYSTEMS
LONDON AND SOUTH-EAST ENGLAND

AN HISTORIC OVERVIEW

PETER WALLER

PEN & SWORD
TRANSPORT

AN IMPRINT OF PEN & SWORD BOOKS LTD.
YORKSHIRE - PHILADELPHIA

British Trolleybus Systems – London and South-East England

First published in Great Britain in 2022 by
Pen and Sword Transport
An imprint of
Pen & Sword Books Ltd.
Yorkshire - Philadelphia

ISBN 978 1 52677 064 6

Typeset in 11/13 Palatino by SJmagic DESIGN SERVICES, India.

Printed and bound by Printworks Global Ltd, London/Hong Kong.

Pen & Sword Books Ltd incorporates the Imprints of Pen & Sword Books Archaeology, Atlas, Aviation,
Battleground, Discovery, Family History, History, Maritime, Military, Naval, Politics, Railways, Select,
Transport, True Crime, Fiction, Frontline Books, Leo Cooper, Praetorian Press, Seaforth Publishing,
Wharncliffe and White Owl.

For a complete list of Pen & Sword titles please contact

PEN & SWORD BOOKS LIMITED
47 Church Street, Barnsley, South Yorkshire, S70 2AS, England
E-mail: enquiries@pen-and-sword.co.uk
Website: www.pen-and-sword.co.uk

or

PEN AND SWORD BOOKS
1950 Lawrence Rd, Havertown, PA 19083, USA
E-mail: Uspen-and-sword@casematepublishers.com
Website: www.penandswordbooks.com

CONTENTS

ABBREVIATIONS

ADC	Associated Daimler Co
AEC	Associated Equipment Co
BAMC	Blackburn Aeroplane & Motor Co Ltd
BCT	Bradford City Tramways
BET	British Electric Traction
BRCW	Birmingham Railway Carriage & Wagon Co Ltd
BTA	Bradford Trolleybus Association
BTH	British Thomson-Houston
BTS	British Trolleybus Society
BUT	British United Traction
Dodson	Christopher Dodson Ltd
EE	English Electric
EMB	Electro-Mechanical Brake Co Ltd
GEC	General Electric Co
GRCW	Gloucester Railway Carriage & Wagon Co Ltd
HN	Hurst Nelson
LCC	London County Council
LCT	Leeds City Tramways
LGOC	London General Omnibus Co
LMS	London, Midland & Scottish Railway
LRTL	Light Railway Transport League
LTHS	Leeds Transport Historical Society
LUT	London United Tramways
MCCW	Metropolitan-Cammell Carriage & Wagon Co Ltd
MET	Metropolitan Electric Tramways
MTMS	Manchester Transport Museum Society
NCB	Northern Coachbuilders Ltd
NTA	National Trolleybus Association
PR	Park Royal
RET	RET Construction Co Ltd
Roe	Charles H. Roe Ltd
RS&J	Ransomes, Sims & Jefferies
RTS	Reading Transport Society (later British Trolleybus Society)
South Met	South Metropolitan Electric Tramways & Lighting Co
TRTB	Teesside Railless Traction Board
UCC	United Construction & Finance Co
UDC	Urban District Council

ACKNOWLEDGEMENTS

This is one of four volumes that, between them, cover all of the trolleybus operators of the British Isles. The majority of the images used are drawn from the collection of the Online Transport Archive, which is a registered charity devoted to the preservation and conservation of images of primarily transport interest. Further information about the archive can be found at its website: www.onlinetransportarchive.org. I am grateful to the following for additional images and, in certain cases, for reading through and making comment on part or all of the manuscript: Colin Barker, Tony Fox, Dave Hall, Philip Kirk, Geoff Lumb, Mike Maybin and Hugh Taylor. It goes without saying that any errors are those of the author and please let him know via the publishers so that these can be corrected in any second or subsequent editions of the books.

INTRODUCTION

This is one of four volumes that will examine the history of all of the trolleybus operators in the British Isles. This one describes those operators based in northern England, Scotland and Northern Ireland.

Although the history of the trolleybus stretches back to early experiments in 1882 undertaken by Ernst Werner Siemens in Berlin it was not until the first decade of the twentieth century that interest in the British Isles was first to emerge. By this time the familiar system of parallel overhead wires with rigid trolleypoles, as pioneered by Max Schiemann in 1904, had come to dominate although there were other systems – such as the Cedes-Stoll, Lloyd-Kohler and Filovia – that also had their exponents and were to influence the development of a number of – short-lived – British systems. Before the introduction of trolleybuses to a number of British operators, delegations, particularly in the early days, travelled to Europe to see this new type of transport in operation.

Although Bradford and Leeds had the honour of opening Britain's first public trolleybus services in June 1911, there had been a number of experimental uses of the trolleybus prior to that date. An earlier generation of public transport – the tramway – had been established through a legislative framework following the Tramways Act of 1870 and much of the development of the trolleybus was also influenced by the law. The 1870 Act made the tramway operator responsible for the maintenance of the road surface stretching to a distance of eighteen inches outside the outer running rail on both sides and, for a period, there was a possibility that a similar cost burden might have been laid on trolleybus operators. This would undoubtedly have made most trolleybus installations prohibitively expensive and thus weakened the case for their introduction. Ironically, however, it was the state of these ill-maintained roads allied to the use of solid-tyred vehicles that represented the Achilles' heel for many of the early operators and led to many early casualties. Although the pneumatic tyre had been originally developed in the 1880s, it was not until the late 1920s that they were routinely fitted to trolleybuses.

When the trolleybus first appeared on Britain's streets there was no concept that it might replace the tram. The trolleybus represented a low-cost means of supplementing existing tram services on lightly trafficked routes and to provide links to communities that were not well served by existing services. There was also a belief that, in certain cases, the introduction of a trolleybus service would be a useful guide to potential traffic and thus be used as a precursor to the introduction of trams. The seating capacity of the new vehicles was severely limited – the first two vehicles in Bradford, for example, could accommodate twenty-eight seated passengers each – when a contemporary double-deck tram's capacity was double that. Moreover, fitted with conventional tramway controllers, trolleybuses were also cumbersome to drive.

It was the development of the first two fully-enclosed double-deck trolleybuses – Nos 521 and 522 – by Bradford Corporation in 1920 and 1922 that established, for the first time, the trolleybus as a serious competitor to the tram. For Britain's tramway operators, which had emerged from the First World War with a backlog of track and overhead maintenance allied to increasingly aged trams, the trolleybus seemed an ideal compromise for replacing the trams: they made use of much of the existing infrastructure – such as the output from the local power station – whilst were cheaper to operate and maintain. The pivotal point here was the decision in Birmingham to convert the Nechells tram route to trolleybus operation; when trolleybuses were introduced on 27 November 1922, this was the first service where trams had been supplanted. Over the succeeding months, a number of delegations visited Birmingham to see the Nechells route in operation and many of these subsequently adopted the trolleybus.

Although a significant number of operators looked at the possibility of introducing trolleybuses, the actual number of operators that made the trolleybus their primary means of public transport was limited. In his, ultimately futile, attempt to dissuade Cardiff Corporation from adopting the trolleybus, William Forbes the general manager came up with some telling statistics in the mid-1930s. He noted that seventy-four tramway systems had been abandoned between September 1931 and September 1937; of these, only eleven had adopted the trolleybus. Moreover, ten trolleybus systems had been converted to motorbus in the period since 1925. The adoption by the London Passenger Transport Board of the trolleybus for its tramway conversion programme was perhaps crucial in maintaining the viability of the trolleybus as a commercially attractive replacement (just as a generation later, the decision to phase the trolleybus out of service in the Metropolis probably sounded its death-knell).

The role of the individual cannot be overstated in the development of the trolleybus. Bradford was fortunate in that both Christopher John Spencer and his successor Richard Henry Wilkinson, appointed when the former moved to London (and played a pivotal role in the development of electric transport there subsequently), were both keen exponents of the trolleybus. Another similar figure was Charles Owen Silver, the general manager at Wolverhampton, who oversaw the development of the trolleybus network. Sometimes – as in the case of William Forbes at Cardiff and Stuart Pilcher at Manchester – the powers that be went over the opposition of the manager to see the introduction of trolleybuses. Later on, it was the vision, for example, of Chaceley Thornton Humpidge at Bradford and Ronald Edgley Cox at Walsall that saw some of the longer surviving systems prosper when others were being abandoned. However, for each Humpidge and Cox there were multiple figures like John C. Wake (who oversaw the conversions of both St Helens and Nottingham and was general manager at Bradford at the crucial time in 1961/62 when the future of the system was under active debate in the light of city centre redevelopment).

That the Bradford system was faced by redevelopment was an irony in terms of the trolleybus; when first introduced, the vehicles were perceived as a flexible alternative to the inflexible tram. Indeed, many early promotional photographs were designed to show this by recording vehicles undertaking dramatic overtaking movements. However, the trolleybus was still restricted, for the most part (the use of traction batteries by some operators gave some better flexibility) by its use of overhead; when one-way systems were developed or when city centres underwent wholesale redevelopment, replacement was costly. This led, in a certain number of cases, to the anachronistic – and generally short-term – operation of contraflow trolleybuses along new one-way streets. Moreover, the pressure for the construction of new housing estates in the suburbs – both to cater for slum clearance and for a growing population – meant that these were beyond the existing termini and were much more easily served by the motorbus.

One factor in the enthusiasm of many operators to adopt the trolleybus was the fact that many councils and companies also owned the power stations that generated the electricity used. There was a virtue in supporting your local power station – what today would be called vertical integration – and public transport provided a demand that made the generating of power more efficient. All this, however, was to change on 13 August 1947 when Royal Assent was given to the Electricity Act 1947. This Act saw the creation of the British Electricity Authority and, on 1 April 1948, more than 500 local authority and company owned electricity undertaking were vested into the newly Nationalised industry. There were exceptions; it was not until 1958, for example that Glasgow Corporation's Pinkston power station ceased to be municipally owned. There were two immediate consequences of the changed ownership and neither worked to the trolleybuses' advantage. Firstly, no longer could the general managers of the transport department and electricity department sit down and agree a price for the electricity used; in the future the trolleybus operators had to pay the market price. Secondly, the price of electricity rose inexorably, making the cheap diesel used by the motorbus all the more attractive.

By the 1960s, the number of suppliers of new trolleybuses had declined to only two, BUT and Sunbeam. Daimler supplied no further trolleybus chassis to British operators after the delivery of batches to Glasgow and Rotherham during 1950 and 1951. Guy Motors Ltd manufactured the last Guy-badged trolleybuses during 1949 and 1950 with a batch of 8ft 0in wide vehicles supplied – appropriately – to Wolverhampton Corporation; however, having acquired the Sunbeam Trolleybus Co Ltd in October 1948 (and closing its Moorfield Works five years later), Guy continued to produce Sunbeam-badged trolleybuses until 1966 although none were supplied to the British market after the delivery of Nos 295-303 to Bournemouth during 1962. These were the last first-generation trolleybuses supplied to any British operator. British United Traction Ltd (BUT) was a joint venture between AEC and Leyland established in 1946. Production was based, until 1948 (when due to declining demand the factory was closed), at Leyland's Kingston factory; thereafter double-deck production was based at Southall and single-deck at Leyland. Subsequently, some work was undertaken at the ex-Crossley works at Stockport. Production continued until 1964 but, by that date, the only orders were for the export market. One factor in the demise of the domestic market was the ready supply of second-hand vehicles as relatively new vehicles were disposed by some of the early post-war conversions; whilst this undoubtedly benefited operators such as Bradford and Walsall, who were able to strengthen their fleets at moderate cost, it did little to sustain the supply base.

It was not only the vehicle suppliers that disappeared; the surviving trolleybus operators needed a regular supply of replacement overhead and fittings. The decision of British Insulated Callender's Cables Ltd (BICC), one of the country's leading supplies of overhead equipment, to cease its production in the late 1960s was another factor in the final demise of the trolleybus. It became increasingly difficult to obtain spares and the condition of the overhead and trolleybuses with many fleets was poor towards their final closure. The lack of spares was often a reason cited for accelerating the final conversion, although when the author was involved in helping to recover the surviving spares from Thornbury depot following Bradford's final conversion in March 1972, there seemed to be a veritable Aladdin's Cave of fittings emerging.

Four systems survived into the 1970s; in the case of Cardiff, it more limped than survived as public services had ceased in December 1969 and only final tours operated in January 1970. Walsall had been subsumed into the West Midlands Passenger Transport Executive and whilst Edgley Cox had a senior role within the new body, it was unlikely that the trolleybus would survive long within a predominantly bus-based business. The transfer of ex-Birmingham buses saw the final elimination in two phases during 1970. The Teesside Railless Traction Board had also been integrated into a larger body – Teesside Municipal Transport – and, despite having opened the country's last extension on 31 March 1968 and having purchased five relatively new vehicles second-hand from Reading, was to be converted in April 1971.

This left Bradford – a case of the first also being the last. In June 1971, the sixtieth anniversary of the system was celebrated. This was a much more low-key event than that which marked the fiftieth anniversary in 1961. The mood was sombre as already moves were afoot for the final conversions. Although there had been no conversions since the Wakefield Road routes were replaced by motorbuses in 1967, the Allerton route – the city's first tram-to-trolleybus conversion (in 1929) and by that date the oldest surviving trolleybus route in the country – was converted to bus operation in February 1971. Over the next twelve months, the remainder of the system disappeared until – come March 1972 – only two routes remained operational. The final weekend – Friday 24 to Sunday 26 March – saw vast numbers of enthusiasts descend on the city to pay their final respects. Was that the end of the story? It might not have been had circumstances been different. The first oil crisis of the early 1970s highlighted the vulnerability of relying on imported oil – just as the Suez Crisis had done in 1956 – and the newly created West Yorkshire Metropolitan County Council did much to try and build a case for a new system. If plans had been carried through, the first routes to have seen trolleybuses restored as part of the council's policy would have been the services to Wibsey and Buttershaw. These plans came to nought as did plans a decade or so later to reintroduce trolleybuses to Leeds as a low-cost alternative to a rapid transit scheme.

The 'K3' (see page 76) and 'P1' classes were the last two batches of pre-war standard trolleybuses to be delivered to London. The 'K3' class were all delivered by the end of November 1940 with delivery of the twenty-five strong 'P1' class, Nos 1697-1721, being completed by September 1941. Here No 1705 is pictured outside the Ram Inn, Wandsworth, whilst heading to Clapham Junction with a service on route 628. By 1954, with the exception of No 1720 that was based briefly at Clapton and Lea Bridge between 1955 and 1957, the entire 'P1' class was allocated to Edmonton and Hammersmith. All were withdrawn during 1960 and 1961. *J. E. Gready/John Meredith Collection/Online Transport Archive*

AUTHOR'S NOTE

Within the specifications for each volume, each system history can only be a brief resume of the story; there are an increasing number of highly-detailed fleet histories and details of many of these can be found in the bibliography. Throughout the book, I have referred to 'trolleybuses'; in the early history they were often referred to as 'tracklesses' or 'trackless trams' whilst a further alternative was 'trolley vehicles'. For the sake of consistency, I have used the word 'trolleybus' throughout except when citing contemporary documentation when the original wording has been maintained. The maps are purely indicative of each network; one of the factors that made trolleybuses a popular alternative to the tram was the relative ease of erecting overhead and so many junctions and roads, particularly in town or city centres, varied over time. The maps thus show all roads that had – at some stage – trolleybus overhead; as a result, more complex systems will show sections that were not operated simultaneously. For example, with Bradford, the routes to Bolton Woods and Frizinghall, both closed in the early 1930s, are shown alongside routes such as those to Buttershaw, Holme Wood and Wibsey that opened between 1955 and 1960. There is a similar issue with route numbers; many operators did not use route letters or number originally and over a period of time the routes that did operate could change both in terms of termini and route number. The photographs used in this book have come from a variety of sources. Wherever possible, contributors have been identified, although some images may have been used without the correct attribution, and every effort made to try and identify current copyright holders in the event of the original photographer being deceased. In the event of any incorrect attribution, apologies are offered and full credit will be given in any future edition. Should this be the case, please make contact with author via the publishers.

Class L2 No 954 was London Transport's second chassisless trolleybus. Delivered in March 1938 it was allocated to Holloway depot where it spent the first nineteen years of its life. In early 1957 it was transferred to Finchley depot and, in this view at Manor House in March 1961, it is working on the 521 route to Holborn Circus. No 954 was immediately distinguishable to staff and enthusiasts by the fact that it was the only standard trolleybus to have a cream band below its windscreen. No 954 enjoyed a long life, not being withdrawn until April 1961. *Fred Ivey*

BOURNEMOUTH

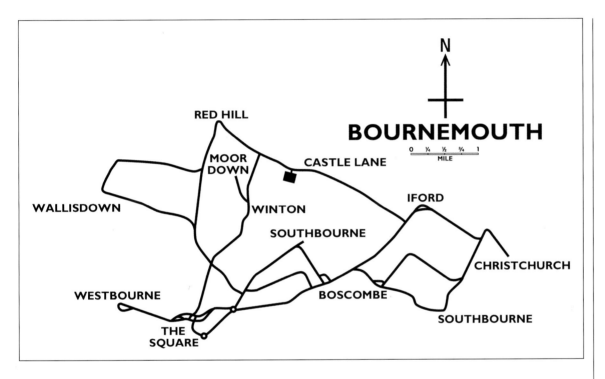

A network of 3ft 6in gauge trams served Bournemouth and Poole; the former operated by the corporation from first opening on 23 July 1902 whilst the latter were initially owned by the Poole & District Tramways Co, a subsidiary of BET, from opening on 6 April 1901 until 15 June 1903, when they were taken over by Poole Corporation. Operation of the Poole system was leased to Bournemouth Corporation from June 1905. There were to be no further tramway extensions after 1906, by which date the total length of tramways operated by Bournemouth Corporation was almost twenty-two route miles.

There were, however, areas ill-served by the trams and the first proposals for alternative means of transport provision emerged in the years before the First World War. In 1910 the first proposal to adopt a 'railless electric traction service' service on a route between Boscombe Pier and Boscombe Arcade was made although nothing other than an interest in watching the future development resulted at that stage.

More serious was the emergence of two new schemes in 1913; these resulted in the depositing of two Bills in parliament: the Bournemouth District Railless Traction Bill for a route along Charminster Road and the Poole, Sandbanks & Westbourne Railless Traction Bill for two routes. Neither Bill was to be enacted – Bournemouth Corporation provided a new motorbus service in place of the former and the outbreak of the First World War delayed the latter – and it was to be a further decade before a trolleybus first appeared in the town.

This was a demonstration – using a skate and the tram track and overhead – using a Trackless Cars chassis fitted with an Olympia sixty-four-seat body in Southcote Road depot; this vehicle was eventually to become Leeds Corporation No 513 two years later.

As elsewhere, the 1920s marked a watershed for Bournemouth as its tramway became increasingly life-expired and its fleet of open-top tramcars dated (as a result of the 3ft 6in gauge, the Board of Trade refused to sanction top covers on the trams even though the fleet had been modernised by the purchase of 40 new trams between 1921 and 1926). There was also the issue of the lease of the Poole system, which was due to expire in 1935. On 1 August 1930, the Bournemouth Corporation Act was given the Royal Assent. The Act saw the enlargement of the borough's boundaries and also permitted the conversion of the Bournemouth trams routes – but not those in Poole – to trolleybus operation along with the conversion of certain motorbus routes as well. The powers were further reinforced by the Bournemouth Corporation (Trolley Vehicles) Order Confirmation Act, which received the Royal Assent on 26 May 1938; this Act was designed 'to *confirm* a Provisional *Order* made by the Minister of Transport under the Bournemouth Corporation Act, 1930, relating to Bournemouth Trolley Vehicles.'

With the local branch of Austin Reed in the background – a building that still exists albeit now under different occupation – on the corner of Gervis Place and Westover Road, No 81 is pictured on a service towards Fishermans Walk. The vehicle was one of six Sunbeam MS2s that were delivered in 1934 that were the last new trolleybuses acquired by Bournemouth Corporation fitted with bodies supplied by English Electric. All were withdrawn between 1952 and 1958. Route 23 was renumbered 37 in March 1956. *R.W.A. Jones/Online Transport Archive*

With the powers to operate trolleybuses in place and following an inspection of the Wolverhampton service, the go-ahead was given for the creation of an experimental one-mile route from Westbourne to The Square. This commenced operation on 13 May 1933, having been inspected officially by the Ministry of Transport earlier the same day, using four hired vehicles; these were later purchased, being numbered 68-71, and included the only single-decker trolleybus operated by Bournemouth (it was to be sold to South Shields in 1942). The four vehicles were based at Southcote Road, travelling to and from the depot using a skate along with the tram track and overhead.

The success of the experimental service resulted in the corporation deciding in early October 1933 that the tram system be converted to trolleybus operation over a three-year period. The first tram to trolleybus conversion occurred on 22 June 1934 when trolleybuses took over the service from Westbourne to Ashley Road. The process of converting the system was more rapid than originally anticipated, with the final tram – on the service to Christchurch – operating on 8 April 1936. The tram services in Poole last operated at the end of the lease on 8 June 1935; services in Poole were thereafter provided by the motorbuses of Hants & Dorset although Bournemouth had proposed their conversion to trolleybus operation.

Having four different types of trolleybus for the experimental service, Bournemouth decided to concentrate on the Sunbeam MS2 chassis for its conversion programme; although the original Sunbeam – No 68 – had been bodied by Weymann, the choice for the majority of new Sunbeams delivered between 1934 and 1936 was Park Royal. No 76 was one of the first deliveries – Nos 72-77 – that were new in 1934. All were taken out of service between 1951 and 1953 following the arrival of the BUT 9641Ts in 1950. *Harry Luff/Online Transport Archive*

In 1935 Bournemouth took delivery of 36 Sunbeam MS2s – Nos 90-125 – to facilitate the tram-to-trolleybus conversion programme. One of the batch – No 112 – was converted to open-top in 1958 and renumbered 202. Withdrawals of the type commenced in 1951 but fifteen survivors were renumbered 209-23 in 1959; the last survivors were withdrawn in 1963. Pictured on 8 September 1960 in Christchurch is No 215; this had originally been No 106 and was one of those to survive into 1963. Two of the batch – open-top No 202 and No 212 – survive in preservation. *C. Carter/Online Transport Archive*

No 149 was the last of a batch of Sunbeam MS2s – Nos 126-49 – that were new during 1935 and 1936. It is pictured here awaiting departure from the Square with a service on route 27 to Moordown; the image predates March 1956 as that month saw the service renumbered 34. This was one of the routes converted to bus operation on 29 September 1963. The surviving members of the batch, which did not include No 149 (withdrawn in 1959), were renumbered 219-26 in 1959 although Nos 130 and 137 were withdrawn before being physically renumbered. *R.W.A. Jones/Online Transport Archive*

FISHERMAN'S WALK
CRANLEIGH ROAD
TUCKTON BRIDGE
22B

Devoid of driver, No 164 awaits departure with a service on route 22B towards Tuckton Bridge; this service was renumbered 23 in 1956. No 164 was one of a second batch of twenty-four Sunbeam MS2s fitted with fifty-six-seat Park Royal bodywork – Nos 150-73 – that were new in 1936. Two of the batch – Nos 157 and 160 – were rebuilt as open-toppers in 1958 and renumbered 200 and 201 respectively at the same time. Withdrawals of the type commenced in 1951 – No 164 was a relatively early casualty being taken out of service in 1957 – with the survivors being renumbered 227-33 in 1959 (although No 152 was withdrawn without being physically renumbered). The last of the type were withdrawn during 1964. *Harry Luff/ Online Transport Archive*

During the period from 1934 to 1936, a total of 102 Sunbeam MS2s fitted with predominantly Park Royal bodywork were delivered; these were housed at the ex-tram depots at Moordown and Southcote Road; a third depot – Pokesdown – which had been downgraded, was restored as an operational depot in 1940. The opening of the new Mallard Road depot and works on 23 July 1953 saw the closure of Moordown depot and the transfer of some of the workshop facilities from Southcote Road. Southcote Road and Pokesdown depots were finally to be closed in 1965 and 1967 respectively.

By the outbreak of war in September 1939, the Bournemouth system extended over almost 33½ route miles. the Second World War saw a number of Bournemouth trolleybuses loaned to other operators, including London (see page 77), Newcastle, Walsall and Wolverhampton as well as the extensions along Barrack Road, linking the Iford Bridge and Christchurch routes, that opened on 22 July 1943 and that between Iford Bridge and Jumpers Corner that opened on 7 August 1944.

The first new trolleybuses acquired by Bournemouth after the Second World War were twenty-four BUT 9641Ts fitted with Weymann fifty-six-seat bodywork; Nos 200-23 were new during 1950 and 1951 and facilitated the last significant service extensions as well as the withdrawal of some of the pre-war vehicles. The batch was renumbered 234-57 during 1958 and 1959 and ten of the batch – Nos 234-43 – were modified to accommodate sixty-eight seated passengers during 1962 and 1963. Typical of the batch post-renumbering is No 244 pictured in The Square with a service on route 25. The vehicles were withdrawn during 1965 and 1966 – No 244 succumbing during the latter year – with No 246 being preserved. *Frank Hunt/LRTA (London Area) Collection/Online Transport Archive*

After the war came a number of further extensions; the last significant addition opening on 15 October 1951 which saw trolleybuses running along Castle Lane to serve a new housing estate at Strouden. With the post-war extensions allied to twenty-four BUT 9641Ts delivered in 1950, the Bournemouth system had reached its maximum extent – some thirty-nine route miles operated by 127 vehicles – although the first withdrawals (other than the single-decker) saw a number of the pre-war fleet, including the surviving three experimental vehicles of 1933, withdrawn following the delivery of the BUTs.

On 31 August 1955 there was a change in the power supply as the transport department ceased to generate its own power at Southcote Road and decided to source the current from the Southern Electricity Board. As the board increased prices over subsequent years, this affected the economics of the system adversely.

In 1955 it was agreed to purchase twenty new Sunbeam MF2Bs with Weymann bodywork; this order was increased by ten in 1957 and Nos 258-87 were delivered during 1958 and 1959. Bournemouth also took advantage of the demise of the Brighton network to purchase seven of that system's post-war BUT 9611Ts in 1959. The new arrivals

On 30 August 1966, Sunbeam MF2B No 267 is pictured in The Square heading towards Boscombe and Southbourne. This was one of thirty 30ft 0in long Sunbeams – Nos 258-87 that were delivered during 1958 and 1959 in order to replace a number of the life-expired vehicles. They were all fitted with Weymann bodywork; initially Nos 258, 259 and 261-69 had accommodation for sixty-two seated passengers, but this was later amended to sixty-three in line with the rest of the batch. All were withdrawn between 1966 and 1969, with No 286 being secured for preservation. *Alan Murray-Rust/Online Transport Archive*

allowed for the withdrawal of the bulk of the surviving pre-war Sunbeams. A final batch of nine Sunbeam MF2Bs were delivered during 1962; these were to be the last new first-generation trolleybuses built for operation in Britain.

By the time that Nos 295-303 were delivered, the future of the system was in doubt. The tide had turned against the trolleybus nationwide and the corporation was faced by the same issues that other operators had encountered: the difficulties in obtaining spare parts; the drift of the population to the suburbs (beyond the existing trolleybus termini with the consequent decline in passenger traffic on the more central routes); the increasing cost of electricity; and plans for major road schemes in the town centre. There were plans for new extensions to serve the suburbs of Kinson, Northbourne and West Howe as well as replacement of the motorbuses along Richmond Park Road; although powers for these routes existed until 1961, nothing was progressed.

On 16 April 1963, the council decided 'that no further purchases of trolleybuses be made [and] to discontinue the use of trolley vehicles'. The original plan envisaged the conversion programme taking ten years but, in reality, it was completed in about half that time.

The first conversions took place on 30 September 1963 when routes 33, 34 and 36 were converted to bus operation; the removal of the overhead on Lansdowne Road and St Paul's Road also meant that the summer circular route 39 could no longer operate. These conversions resulted in the withdrawal of the last of the pre-war trolleybuses.

Further conversions followed during 1965 and early 1966. The trolleybuses allocated to Southcote Road were transferred to Mallard Road on 7 June 1965. On 25 September 1966, the services that operated up the 1 in 8 gradient of Richmond Hill – the 27, 28, 29, 31 and 32 – were converted to motorbus operation. This resulted in the withdrawal of the 1950 BUTs as well as the first of the 1958 Sunbeams; the latter withdrawals were cannibalised to keep the rest of the type operational.

In the late 1950s, three of the surviving pre-war Sunbeam MS2s – Nos 112, 157 and 160 – were rebuilt as sixty-nine-seat open-toppers and renumbered 202, 200 and 201 respectively. Here No 200 is pictured on 14 June 1964 at Christchurch during a Southern Counties Touring Society tour of the system. Following withdrawal, one of the trio – No 202 – was secured for preservation. *John Meredith/Online Transport Archive*

In addition to the purchase of the new Sunbeam MF2Bs, Bournemouth also entered the second-hand market, taking advantage of the decline of the Brighton system to purchase a total of seven from that system's fleet. Four of the acquisitions were Brighton Corporation Nos 45-48, which became Nos 288-91 in Bournemouth. Here No 291 is pictured outside Southcote Road depot on 15 April 1963. All four were withdrawn during 1965. Southcote Road depot dated back to 1902 and was originally used to accommodate the corporation's 3ft 6in trams – as evinced by the redundant track – but was coming to the end of its life when pictured here; it finally closed in 1965, although the building itself remains extant at the time of writing in commercial use. *Alan Murray-Rust/Online Transport Archive*

Apart from the batch of ex-Brighton Corporation BUT 9611Ts, Bournemouth purchased the three identical vehicles supplied to Brighton, Hove & District in 1948. The three, typified by No 293, were all fitted with Weymann fifty-six-seat bodywork and entered service during 1959. However, their second life was destined to be relatively short, all being withdrawn during 1965. *Frank Hunt/LRTA (London Area) Collection/ Online Transport Archive*

The last new trolleybuses purchased for operation were a further batch of nine Sunbeam MF2Bs that were delivered in 1962; Nos 295-303 represented the last wholly new first-generation trolleybuses delivered to any operator in the British Isles with No 301 being the last to be completed. No 299 – pictured here – was one of the three from the batch to be preserved after withdrawal (the others being Nos 297 and 301). All nine were finally withdrawn after only seven years' service in 1969. *Marcus Eavis/Online Transport Archive*

The end of the Bournemouth system came on 20 1969 when the final batch of services – serving Iford, Southbourne and Christchurch – were converted. The official last trolleybus was No 301. A total of seven Bournemouth trolleybuses survive in preservation. These are two of the pre-war Sunbeams – Nos 99 and 202 (the latter being one of the three converted to open-top form in the late 1950s) – one of the post-war BUTs (No 246) and four of the MF2Bs (Nos 286, 297, 299 and 301).

The final Bournemouth trolleybuses operated on 20 April 1969 and especially decorated to run during the last week, MF2B No 278 is seen on the famous turntable at Christchurch. Although there were rumours that Walsall might acquire some of the relatively new Sunbeam MF2Bs these proved to be ill-founded and all bar four of the thirty-nine were sold for scrap; Nos 286, 297, 299 and 301 were all secured for preservation. *Marcus Eavis/Online Transport Archive*

Fleet number	Registration	Chassis	Body	New	Withdrawn	Notes
68	LJ7701	Sunbeam MS2	Weymann H60R	1933	1952	
69	LJ7702	AEC 663T	EE H60R	1933	1950	Converted to petrol bus 1936
70	LJ7703	AEC 661T	EE H50R	1933	1950	Converted to petrol bus 1936
71	LJ7704	Thornycroft BD	Brush B32C	1933	1942	Sold to South Shields
72-77	AEL4-405	Sunbeam MS2	PR H56D	1934	1951-53	
78-83	AEL406-411	Sunbeam MS2	EE H56D	1934	1951-58	
84-89 (84-86 and 88 renumbered 205-08 1959-60)	ALJ60-65	Sunbeam MS2	PR H56D	1934	1957-63	
90-125 (112 renumbered 202 1958; 90, 93, 97, 99, 101/05/06/17/19/21 renumbered 209-18 1959-60)	ALJ964-999	Sunbeam MS2	PR H56D (202 rebuilt as 69-seat open-top 1958)	1935	1951-65	99 and 202 preserved
126-49 (129-32/37/41/44/47 renumbered 219-26 1959-60)	BEL811-834	Sunbeam MS2	PR H56D	1935-36	1951-65	
150-73 (157 and 160 renumbered 200 and 201 1958; 152/59/62/63/67/68/70 renumbered 227-33 1959-60)	BRU1-24	Sunbeam MS2	PR H56D (157 and 160 rebuilt as 69-seat open-top 1958)	1936	1951-64	
200-23 (renumbered 234-57 1959-60)	KLJ334-357	BUT 9641T	Weymann H56D (234-43 modified to 68 seats 1962-63)	1950	1965-66	212 preserved
258-77	WRU258-277	Sunbeam MF2B	Weymann H63D (258/59/61-69 originally H62D)	1958-59	1966-69	
278-87	YLJ278-87	Sunbeam MF2B	Weymann H63D	1959	1969	286 preserved

Fleet number	Registration	Chassis	Body	New	Withdrawn	Notes
288-91	HUF45-48	BUT 9611T	Weymann H56R	1948	1965	Ex-Brighton 45-48; acquired 1959
292-94	DNK992-994	BUT 9611T	Weymann H56D	1948	1965	Ex-BHD 6391-93; acquired 1959
295-303	295-303LJ	Sunbeam MF2B	Weymann H63D	1962	1969	287, 299 and 301 preserved

Route number	From	To	Date Opened	Date Closed	Notes
20	Square	Christchurch (via Jumpers)	22 July 1943	19 April 1969	
21	Square	Christchurch (via Southbourne)	8 April 1936	19 April 1969	
21A	Westbourne	Christchurch (via Southbourne)	8 April 1936	25 February 1940	
22	Square	Southbourne	23 December 1935	19 April 1969	
22	Southbourne	Tuckton Bridge	1 December 1946	19 April 1969	
22A	Westbourne	Tuckton Bridge (via Southbourne)	10 April 1947	3 October 1948	
22B (23 from March 1956)	Square	Tuckton Bridge (via Cranleigh Road)	16 August 1948	19 April 1969	
23	Square	Fisherman's Walk	21 November 1935	21 September 1953	
23A	Westbourne	Fisherman's Walk	1 January 1936	30 September 1937	
24	Square	Iford Bridge	25 March 1935	19 April 1969	
24	Iford Bridge	Jumpers Corner	7 August 1944	19 April 1969	
24A	Westbourne	Iford Bridge	25 March 1935	31 October 1937	
25	Square	Boscombe (via Holdenhurst Road)	22 June 1934	31 October 1937	

Route number	From	To	Date Opened	Date Closed	Notes
25A (25 from March 1956)	Westbourne	Boscombe (via Holdenhurst Road)	22 June 1934	12 September 1965	
25B	Westbourne	Fisherman's Walk (via Holdenhurst Road)	28 July 1938	25 February 1940	
26	Square	Moordown	7 June 1935	5 March 1966	Central terminus relocated to the Triangle from the Square on 30 March 1947
26	Moordown	Lawford Road	15 April 1937	5 March 1966	Central terminus relocated to the Triangle from the Square on 30 March 1947
26A (27 from March 1956)	Square	West Way (via Moordown)	19 October 1938	25 September 1966	Central terminus relocated to the Triangle from the Square on 30 March 1947
27 (34 from March 1956)	Square	Moordown (via Lansdowne)	28 June 1935	29 September 1963	
27 (34 from March 1956)	Moordown	Lawford Road	11 March 1937	29 September 1963	
28	Square	Broadway Hotel (via Five Ways)	25 August 1935	25 September 1966	Central terminus relocated to the Triangle from the Square on 30 March 1947
28A (29 from March 1956)	Square	West Way via Five Ways and Broadway)	19 October 1938	25 September 1966	Central terminus relocated to the Triangle from the Square on 30 March 1947
29 (35 from March 1956)	Square	Malvern Road (via Five Ways)	5 April 1937	4 April 1965	Central terminus relocated to the Triangle from the Square on 30 March 1947
30	Square	Columbia Road (via Wallisdown)	15 April 1938	16 April 1966	Central terminus relocated to the Triangle from the Square on 30 March 1947
30A (31 from March 1956)	Square	Columbia Road (via Ensbury Park)	8 April 1939	25 September 1966	Central terminus relocated to the Triangle from the Square on 30 March 1947

Route number	From	To	Date Opened	Date Closed	Notes
31	Triangle	Triangle (via Five Ways, Strouden and Boscombe)	15 October 1951	11 October 1953	Section along Castle Lane serving new housing estate at Strouden was the last major extension
32	Square	Triangle (via Boscombe, Strouden and Five Ways)	15 October 1951	11 October 1953	
31 (32 from March 1956)	Triangle	Iford (via Five Ways and Strouden)	12 October 1953	25 September 1966	
33	Winton	Holdenhurst Road (via Strouden)	23 May 1953	28 September 1963	
33	Holdenhurst Road	Iford (via Triangle and Winton)	23 May 1953	28 September 1963	
34 (36 from March 1956)	Lansdowne	Columbia Road (via Ensbury Park)	5 June 1954	29 September 1963	
35	Bournemouth Pier	Fisherman's Walk	16 April 1954	5 April 1956	
36	Lansdowne	Columbia Road	17 September 1956	28 September 1963	
37	Bournemouth Square	Fisherman's Walk	21 November 1935	30 September 1963	
38	Bournemouth pier circular via Boscombe	Bournemouth pier	30 March 1956	23 August 1964	Operated by open-top trolleybuses
39	Bournemouth Pier	Bournemouth Pier (circular route)	24 May 1958	29 September 1963	

One of the more familiar landmarks on the Bournemouth system was Tuckton Bridge, with its restrictions. With the notice warning drivers that trolleybuses must not pass on the bridge and that the maximum speed across the structure was 10mph prominent in the foreground, No 296 makes its way onto the bridge on 5 April 1969. One of the nine MF2Bs delivered during 1969, No 296 was not one of the trio that made it into preservation. *Geoffrey Tribe/Online Transport Archive*

BRIGHTON

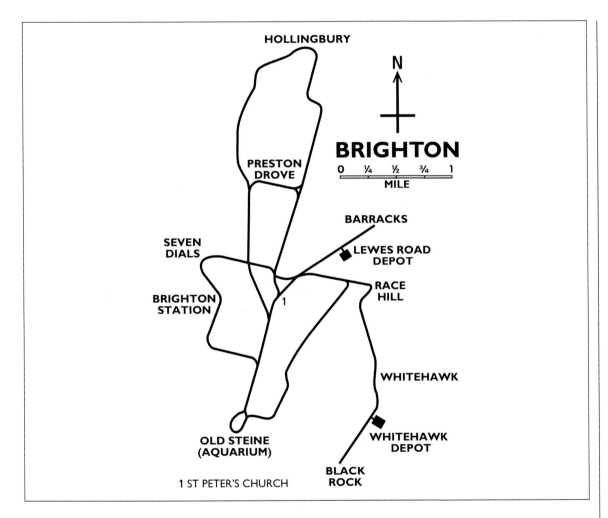

HOLLINGBURY

N

BRIGHTON

0   ¼   ½   ¾   1
MILE

PRESTON
DROVE

BARRACKS

SEVEN
DIALS

LEWES ROAD
DEPOT

RACE
HILL

BRIGHTON
STATION

1

WHITEHAWK

OLD STEINE
(AQUARIUM)

WHITEHAWK
DEPOT

BLACK
ROCK

1 ST PETER'S CHURCH

By the mid-1930s, Brighton Corporation was operating a compact network of 3ft 6in gauge trams; although restrictions meant that the fleet could only comprise open-top trams, there had been a programme of steady replacement with thirty-five rebodied trams entering service between 1932 and 1937.

However, both Brighton and neighbouring Hove had been the scene of early trolleybus experiments. In 1909, Brighton council contemplated the introduction of trolleybuses although nothing progressed whilst, in 1910, two companies promoted schemes; the BET-backed Brighton District Tramway envisaged a tramway linking Brighton with Worthing along with a trolleybus service within the town whilst the Brighton, Hove & Preston United Omnibus Co sought powers for a trolleybus service linking Worthing with Rottingdean via Brighton. Without the backing of the local road-owning authorities,

Initially Brighton and Hove councils seemed to be co-operating in the development of a trolleybus service between the two communities; however, plans to seek powers for a joint system were rejected by Hove. Both councils, however, decided to undertake experimental services within their boundaries. Whilst Brighton opted for a conventional system using a double-deck vehicle the Railless Electric Traction Co had demonstrated in Leeds, Hove decided to test the Cedes-Stoll system and acquired a single vehicle in 1914 that was fitted with a Dodson-built thirty-three-seat open-top double-deck body. Test operation of the vehicle commenced on a route between Hove station and Church Road via Goldstone Villas and George Street on 18 September 1914. The test ended later the same year and, although Brighton persisted with attempts to try and introduce a service, circumstances during the First World War and an inability to agree meant that these early proposals came to nought. *D.W.K. Jones Collection/Online Transport Archive*

In January 1936, prior to the introduction of trolleybuses to Brighton, London Transport No 61, which had previously been displayed at Bournemouth, was displayed at The Level, just north of St Peter's Church, on the occasion of a referendum held on 8 January to determine the future of public transport in the town. It bore a poster promoting 'Trolleybuses for Brighton' with the legend, below the lower deck windows, proclaiming 'The latest type of this trolleybus is free from wireless interference'. It is seen here alongside Class E tram No 69; this was one of a trio of trams produced between 1929 and 1931. Production of largely similar open-top tramcars continued through until 1937, all of which had less than a decade in service before their withdrawal in 1939 as the tramways were replaced by trolleybuses. *D.W.K. Jones Collection/Online Transport Archive*

these parliamentary Bills struggled and were heavily amended and that proposed by BET failed to be enacted. That promoted by the Brighton, Hove & Preston United Omnibus Co received the Royal Assent on 2 August 1911 but only for the section from Rottingdean to Ovingdean and nothing was progressed thereafter.

Whilst the two company Bills were being mangled other plans started to develop; from early September 1911, representatives of Brighton and Hove councils discussed the possibility of a trolleybus service linking the two – this was officially noted by Brighton on 26 October 1911 – with plans for both to deposit Bills for powers to operate trolleybuses in their areas. However, then Hove Council decided not to proceed with trolleybuses; this decision was reversed and, in early 1912, both councils introduced Bills to parliament and, on 7 August 1912, both the Brighton Corporation Act 1912 and the Hove Corporation Act 1912 received the Royal Assent.

In 1913, following Board of Trade approval, Brighton installed trolleybus overhead along a stretch of London Road; this extended for almost 700 yards between Rosehill Terrace and Trafalgar Road and, after the delivery on 23 December 1913 of an open-top double-decker constructed for the Railless Electric Traction Construction Co Ltd (which had been previously demonstrated in Leeds) test runs over the newly erected trolleybus overhead commenced; this continued through to November 1914 when the tests ceased and the overhead was removed.

Whilst Brighton had gone for the conventional type of overhead, Hove opted for the Cedes-Stoll (as adopted by both Aberdare and Keighley). For test purposes, a stretch of overhead was erected between Church Road and Hove railway station. Hove also received an open-top double-decker – this time with a chassis supplied by Cedes-Stoll with a body built by Christopher Dodson Ltd of Willesden London – with test running commencing on 14 September 1914. The tests again ceased in November 1914. Although Brighton sought to negotiate with Hove over the construction of the through route – even offering to go to arbitration over the choice of equipment – nothing further progressed.

With the failure of the 1913/14 schemes, nothing further – other than desultory proposals in 1925, 1929 and 1935 – the story of the trolleybus in Brighton lay dormant for more than two decades. During 1937, discussions began with the Thomas Tilling-owned Brighton, Hove & District Omnibus Co, which had been formed in November 1935 in succession to the older Brighton, Hove & Preston United Omnibus Co (which dated originally to 1884), over the creation of a revenue pooling scheme. On 29 July 1938 Royal Assent was given to the Brighton Corporation (Transport) Act 1938; the powers contained

The period during which trams and trolleybuses operated alongside each other in Brighton was relatively limited. The last trams operated on 31 August 1939 with the first trolleybuses having been introduced on 1 May 1939. One of the corporation's original batch of AEC 661Ts is pictured here at Aquarium with a tram behind prior to heading north with a service on route 48 to Lewes Road – Brighton's first trolleybus service. *H. Fayle/via John Meredith Collection/Online Transport Archive*

Although the first eight trolleybuses owned by Brighton, Hove & District were delivered in 1939 and actually registered as BPN340-347, they did not enter service until during 1945 and 1946. Identical to the pre-war batch of AEC 661Ts that the corporation acquired in 1939, the eight were initially numbered 6340-47 but were subsequently to be renumbered 340-47. All withdrawn in 1959, No 6340 – which is pictured here at Aquarium on route 42 – was preserved and now forms part of the Science Museum collection and is stored at the museum's Wroughton site alongside Ipswich No 44. *Harry Luff/Online Transport Archive*

within the Act permitted the creation of the revenue-pooling arrangement along with the conversion of the tramway network to trolleybus operation. The new joint working area came into effect on 1 April 1939 – shortly after the retirement of Brighton's general manager William Marsh (who had sought to maintain the tramway network to the highest standards) – and work on the conversion quickly progressed.

The first tram route to be converted – on 26 April 1939 – was that along Dyke Road, which was replaced by motorbus. The first trolleybus service – replacing the tram on the Lewes Road route – commenced operation on 1 May 1939. On 1 June 1939, trolleybuses replaced trams on the Preston Drove (Ditchling Road and Beaconsfield Road) circular service; opened at the same time was a ¾-mile extension along Ditchling Road. The next service to be converted to trolleybus was that to the main station on 17 July 1939; this was extended to Seven Dials and Dyke Road, over part of the former Dyke Road tramway (to supplement the motorbus service introduced in April) to create a new circular service. Following the operation of the final tram on 31 August 1939 – a process originally anticipated to take between three and five years had been completed in less than six months – trolleybuses were introduced to the sections to Race Hill via Elm Grove and to Queens Park Road.

In 1947 the Brighton Corporation fleet was supplemented by the acquisition of six BUT 9611Ts – Nos 45-50 – that were fitted with Weymann bodywork. One of the batch – No 48 – is pictured here outside Lewes Road depot. All were withdrawn in 1959 with four – Nos 45-48 – being sold to Bournemouth (as Nos 288-91) and the remaining two to Bradford (as Nos 802 and 803). Lewes Road depot had its origins as Brighton Corporation's sole tram depot; it originally opened on 25 November 1901 and still in use today by Brighton & Hove Bus & Coaches; the trolleybuses operated by Brighton, Hove & District were based at the company's depot at Black Rock. *Harry Luff/Online Transport Archive*

For the opening of the system, Brighton Corporation took delivery of forty-four AEC 661Ts fitted with Weymann bodywork; the joint area agreement anticipated 20 per cent of the mileage operated by the trolleybuses being operated by Brighton, Hove & District. As a result, the company acquired eight similar vehicles; however, when these were delivered in late 1939 and early 1940, traffic requirements had been reduced as a result of the Second World War and the eight vehicles were stored for the duration of hostilities in the company's Conway Street depot. The corporation-owned vehicles were always based at the former tram depot at Lewes Road. In 1942, the low levels of wartime traffic permitted five of the corporation vehicles to be loaned to Newcastle Corporation.

With the end of hostilities, the expansion of the trolleybus network continued with the opening of the section from Race Hill to Black Road on 3 March 1946; this was designed to serve new housing developments and also passed the company's Whitehawk Road depot – opened originally in 1937 – at which the eight company-owned vehicles were now based.

Recorded in 1959, the year in which the first trolleybus-to-bus conversions were carried out in Brighton, two of the original batch of vehicles – No 31 on the left about to depart on route 26 to Hollingbury and No 20 on the right with a service on route 46 to Preston Drove – stand at the Aquarium terminus. The two services were amongst those that survived through to the final conversion of the system on 30 June 1961 whilst both of the trolleybuses were also to remain operational until that year although twenty of the batch had been withdrawn 1957 and 1960. *Marcus Eavis/Online Transport Archive*

The final development of the Brighton system came with the opening in three stages – from Ditchling Road to Larkfield Way on 28 November 1948, thence to Carden Hill on 23 March 1949 and, finally, from Carden Hill to Preston Drove on 12 August 1951 – to create an outer circular route. Services that headed to Hollingbury on route 46 returned as route 26 and vice versa. In order to operate the new services, the corporation acquired eight new trolleybuses – although two did not enter service until 1953 – and the company three.

Further powers were obtained in the Brighton Corporation (Trolley Vehicles) Order Confirmation Act 1947 and the Brighton Corporation (Trolley Vehicles) Order Confirmation Act 1952, which received the Royal Assent on 31 July 1947 and 1 August 1952 respectively; however, these powers were not exercised. In addition, two sections authorised under the 1938 Act – Balfour Road and Carden Avenue to Ladies Mile Road – were never completed.

In the early 1950s, the first suggestions of trolleybus-to-motorbus conversion arose. These were rejected by the council in 1954 but, two years later, a similar proposal was approved. The situation was made more complicated by the desire to modify the joint traffic agreement to include Southdown; this eventually made effective on 1 January 1961.

HASTINGS

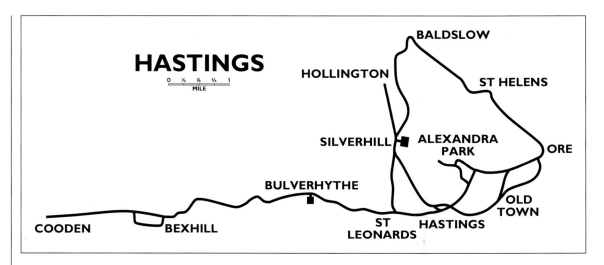

T he Hastings & District Electric Tramways Co Ltd possessed a 3ft 6in gauge tramway; the first section opened on 31 July 1905 and – courtesy of the long coastal route westwards through Bulverhythe to Cooden – extended over more than 19½ route miles. The system had originally developed as two sections and it was not until 12 January 1907 when the two were linked; this new section was unusual in being equipped by the Dolter stud system of current collection – the corporation objected to overhead on the Promenade – but this proved unsuccessful and was replaced by petrol-electric trams in 1914 with conventional overhead only being installed after the First World War.

Like most company-operated tramways, the legislation from 1905 that allowed the tramway's construction in Hastings permitted the corporation to assume ownership and operation. This right could be invoked in 1925 – although the corporation did not take up the option – and from the early 1920s the company examined the future of the tramway. One option was to modernise the fleet; however, the corporation – in an era before bus regulation came in (as a result of the Road Traffic Act 1930) – could not offer protection against unbridled bus competition. With Alfred Baker, the Wolverhampton general manager, providing advice, the company decided to opt for trolleybuses; one factor in this was the company's ownership of its own power station (this was located in Parker Road, Ore; it was sold in 1936 following the take-over of the company by Maidstone & District with the trolleybuses being supplied from the municipal power station thereafter).

Although there was opposition from the corporation, Royal Assent was granted on 29 July 1927 for the Hastings Tramways Company (Trolley Vehicles) Act 1927; this empowered the company to convert its tram routes to trolleybus and undertake a number of extensions. The corporation opposition to the original bill resulted in a clause in the final Act that permitted it and the neighbouring Bexhill-on-Sea to acquire the system in 1945 or every five years thereafter. This was amended by the Hastings Corporation

An undated – but fairly early view – sees two of the original open-top Guy BTXs fitted with Dodson bodywork at the Memorial town clock; that on the left is picking up passengers prior to heading towards Hollington whilst the second is obscured partially by the Memorial itself. A total of eight of these vehicles were acquired during 1928 and 1930. All were withdrawn in 1940 although No 3 was to survive and was restored in 1953. *Barry Cross Collection/Online Transport Archive*

(General Powers) Act 1937, which received the Royal Assent on 13 July 1937, which allowed Hastings to act independently to take-over the operation in 1945 and periodically thereafter whether or not Bexhill participated.

The first conversion – from Hollington to the Fishmarket via Bohemia Road – took place on 1 April 1928; the section from the Memorial and the Fishmarket had not previously been served by tram. This was followed on 21 May 1928 by the introduction of trolleybuses to the Memorial to Silverhill via Esplanade and London Road route. This was followed on 30 July 1928 by the routes from the Memorial to Alexandra Park and from Grand Parade to West Marina; the latter was part of the long route through to Cooden; the remainder of the Cooden route became trolleybus operated on 18 September 1928. This included the use of Bexhill Road in place of the private reservation used by the tram and the conversion of Bulverhythe depot to accommodate trolleybuses; the early fleet had been allocated to the company's other depot at Silverhill. Bulverhythe depot was closed in 1941 with the operations then being based on Silverhill depot alone.

On 24 January 1929, trolleybuses replaced trams on the route from Laton Road to St Helens via Priory Road and Ore. This was followed on 4 March 1929 by the opening of the route from the Fishmarket to Ore via the High Street and Clive Vale. The section from Fishmarket to the Old Market Cross via High Street was never operated by tram but the section from the Old Town to Ore replaced the existing tramway.

The end of the tramway came on 15 May 1929 with the conversion of the route from Silverhill to St Helens via Bladslow. The same day saw the introduction of two short links – from Hollington to a new terminus at Glen Road and from Alexandra Park to Park Cross Road – for which powers did not exist. The position was regularised as a result of the Hastings Tramways Company (Trolley Vehicles) Act 1930, which received the Royal Assent on 10 June 1930. This Act also permitted the construction of a number of extensions; all but one of these were completed and were opened as follows: from Langham Hotel to Park Gates on 10 August 1930; the loop serving Hastings station on 18 January 1931; and, the direct cut-off route in Bexhill on 1 July 1931.

For the operation of the network, the company employed fifty-eight trolleybuses. All were based around the Guy BTX chassis; eight – Nos 1-8 – were open-top double-deckers whilst the remainder – Nos 9-58 – were single-deckers.

The ownership of the company changed on 11 November 1935 when the Hastings Tramways Co became a wholly-owned subsidiary of Maidstone & District Motor Services Ltd, which resulted in a change of livery from brown to green, although there was to be no outward change to the fleet name displayed by the fleet until 30 September 1957 when the Hastings Tramway Co was formally merged into its parent company. The merger was sanctioned by the Hastings Tramways Act 1957, which received the Royal Assent on 31 July 1957

On a postcard franked 7 July 1931 two of the then recently new Guy BTX single-deckers – Nos 14 and 29 – are pictured at the town clock on services to Ore and Hollington respectively. The view must have been relatively recently recorded as trolleybuses only reached Ore on 24 January 1929. A number of these vehicles were sold to Derby, Mexborough & Swinton and Nottingham during the Second World War; No 29 was one of those that went to Mexborough & Swinton. *Barry Cross Collection/Online Transport Archive*

A **total** of fifty single-deck Guy BTXs fitted with Ransomes, Sims & Jefferies thirty-two-seat bodywork were put into service between 1928 and 1930. Of these six were sold to Nottingham in 1941, six to Derby in 1942 and six to Mexborough in Swinton in 1943 as the delivery of twenty AEC 661Ts rendered them surplus to requirements. The last numerically of the batch was No 58, which is seen here inside Silverhill depot towards the end of its life. All of the type were withdrawn by the end of 1955. After withdrawal No 45 was used initially as a ticket office by Maidstone & District; subsequently sold off, the vehicle was secured for preservation in the mid-1970s and is currently under restoration. *Frank Hunt/LRTA (London Area) Collection/Online Transport Archive*

Fleet replacement was now under consideration and new trolleybuses were ordered in 1939. A total of twenty AEC 661Ts were delivered during 1940 out of the forty-eight originally ordered as a result of restrictions imposed by the Second World War. Their arrival allowed for the withdrawal of all of the open-top Guy BTXs – although one was retained in store (it would be restored to operational condition in 1953 as a decorated vehicle to mark the coronation of HM Queen Elizabeth II) – as well as a number of the single-deckers. A number of the latter were sold between 1941 and 1943 to Nottingham, Derby and Mexborough & Swinton to supplement their fleets.

After the war, two batches of Sunbeam Ws were delivered; the ten new in 1946 had semi-Utility bodywork supplied by Park Royal whilst fifteen that arrived in 1948 were bodied by Weymann. These were the last trolleybuses to be acquired by the company. These deliveries allowed for more of the single-deckers to be withdrawn but it was not until 1955 that the last of the batch were taken out of service. That post-war period also saw the final extension to the system when a short extension to the Hollington route saw the route extended 300 yards from Glen Road in order to replace the existing trolley reverser with a loop. This took the total length of the system to just over 22½ route miles.

By 1948, the twelve routes that had operated in 1930 had effectively been reduced to only four; these, however, utilised all of the overhead except for the station and Laton Road loops. The section from London Road into Grand Parade (West) was used for depot workings only whilst the station loop was used for extras.

In neither 1945 nor 1950 did the local authorities exercise their option to take over the system; during 1954, Hastings Corporation expressed some interest in pursuing the option to take over on 30 June 1955. However, despite local support for the trolleybuses, which were profitable, the corporation decided against purchase. Maidstone & District sought to safeguard its position through the Hastings Tramways Act 1957; apart from the aforementioned merger, the Act also permitted the company to replace the trolleybuses with motorbuses.

In August 1958, Maidstone & District announced its intention to convert the system and ordered new motorbuses for the purpose. Although the original plans had been for the last trolleybuses to operate in January 1959, delays in the delivery of the new motorbuses resulted in a temporary reprieve. As a result, the entire system remained operational through until 31 May 1959 although a number of vehicles were withdrawn to be cannibalised for spares over the preceding months. The last service trolleybus was No 28. The following day – 1 June 1959 – saw Nos 3A and 34 used for the official farewell.

After closure, all of AEC 661Ts from 1940 were sold for scrap but the twenty-five post-war Sunbeam Ws all found new homes; twelve were sold to Bradford Corporation, five to Maidstone Corporation and eight to Walsall Corporation. Of these, one of quintet sold to Maidstone – No 34 – was secured for preservation. No 3A was fitted with a diesel engine and also survives in this modified form. In addition, two of the pre-war Guy BTX single-deckers survive: No 45, which was used as a booking office after withdrawal in 1954 and was subsequently rescued, and another – possibly No 46 – was sold via the Ministry of Defence to a veteran for use as a home. The latter is in unrestored condition at Sandtoft.

In 1940 Hastings acquired its first new double-deck trolleybuses since 1930 with two batches of AEC 661Ts delivered. The new arrivals permitted the withdrawal of the original double-deck Guy BTXs and also a number of the single-deckers. The first ten – Nos 1-10 – were bodied by Park Royal and here No 5 is pictured heading towards Hollington with a service on route 11. All of the batch were finally withdrawn in 1959. *Frank Hunt/ LRTA (London Area) Collection/Online Transport Archive*

The second batch of AEC 661Ts delivered in 1940 – Nos 11-20 (such as No 18 illustrated here) – were fitted with fifty-four-seat bodywork supplied by Park Royal. All ten were taken out of service during 1959. *Frank Hunt/LRTA (London Area) Collection/ Online Transport Archive*

The first new trolleybuses that Hastings & District acquired post-war were ten Sunbeam Ws fitted with Park Royal fifty-six-seat bodywork. Nos 21-30 were delivered during 1946 and here No 28 is seen passing the Burton shop whilst heading towards Hollington on route 6. Following withdrawal in 1959, all ten of the batch were sold to Bradford Corporation; unfortunately, their second-hand career was relatively short as a change of policy meant that all were withdrawn for a final time by the end of October 1963. *Frank Hunt/ LRTA (London Area) Collection/Online Transport Archive*

On 25 March 1956 No 35 stands at St Helens prior to heading to Hollington on route 11. No 35 was one of fifteen Sunbeam Ws fitted with Weymann bodywork acquired in 1948 that were the last new trolleybuses purchased by Hastings & District. Following the system's conversion, eight of the batch were sold to Walsall and five – including No 35 – to Maidstone with the remaining two being acquired by Bradford. The quintet sent to Kent were all withdrawn between 1965 and 1967. No 34 was preserved following withdrawal in Walsall in 1970. *Julian Thompson/Online Transport Archive*

In 1952 No 3 – one of the original open-top Guy BTXs fitted with Dodson bodywork – was salvaged from Bulverhythe depot, where it had somehow managed to survive in store since 1938 and restored to as near original condition as possible albeit equipped with lights and bunting. It reappeared in service during the summer of 1953, helping to mark the coronation of Queen Elizabeth II, and was then used each summer until the final closure of the trolleybus network. After closure, the vehicle was fitted with a diesel engine and continued in use. It remains in preservation in this converted form. *LRTA (London Area) Collection/Online Transport Archive*

Fleet number	Registration	Chassis	Body	New	Withdrawn	Notes
1-8	DY4853/4854/ 4965-4970	Guy BTX	Dodson 057ROS	1928-30	1940	3 restored as 3A in 1953; fitted with diesel engine after 1959; 3A preserved
9-58	DY5111-5140/ 5452-5461/ 5576-5585	Guy BTX	RS&J B32C	1928-30	1941-55	Six (9, 18, 19, 24, 40 and 51) to Nottingham 1941; six (Nos 11, 13, 21, 35, 38 and 57) to Derby 1942; six (16, 29, 47, 48. 52 and 53) to Mexborough & Swinton 1943; 45 and 46 preserved
1-10	BDY776-785	AEC 661T	Weymann H54R	1940	1959	
11-20	BDY786-795	AEC 661T	PR H54R	1940	1959	
21-30	BDY796-805	Sunbeam W	PR H56R	1946	1959	All sold to Bradford
31-45	BDY806-820	Sunbeam W	Weymann H56R	1947	1959	Two (40 and 45) sold to Bradford; five (32, 34, 35, 42 and 43) sold to Maidstone; eight (31, 33, 36-39, 41 and 44) sold to Walsall; 34 preserved;

Route number (see separate table)	From	To	Date Opened	Date Closed	Notes
	Hollington	Memorial	1 April 1928	31 May 1959	
	Fish Market	Mcmorial	1 April 1928	31 May 1959	
	Memorial	Silverhill (via London Road and Esplanade)	21 May 1928	31 May 1959	
	Alexandra Park	Memorial	30 July 1928	31 May 1959	
	Grand Parade (London Road)	West Marina	30 July 1928	31 May 1959	
	Cooden	West Marina	18 September 1928	31 May 1959	
	Laton Road	St Helens (via Priory Road and Ore)	24 January 1929	31 May 1959	
	Fish Market	Ore (via Clive Vale)	4 March 1929	31 May 1959	
	St Helens	Silverhill (via Baldslow)	15 May 1929	31 May 1959	
	Hollington	Hollington (Glen Road)	15 May 1929	31 May 1959	
	Alexandra Park	Park Cross Road	15 May 1929	31 May 1959	
	Park Gates	Langham Hotel (via Elphinstone Road)	10 August 1930	31 May 1959	
	Hastings station loop		18 January 1931	31 May 1959	

Route number (see separate table)	From	To	Date Opened	Date Closed	Notes
	Devonshire Road	Cooden Road (via Western Road)	1 July 1931	31 May 1959	Cut-off route in Bexhill
	Hollington (Glen Road)	Hollington loop	1947	31 May 1959	Short extension to permit replacement of reverser by loop

Route number	Details
1	1932 – Circular via Queen's Road and St Helens; 1945 – St Helens to Hollington; c1946 – service ceased
2	1932 – Circular via Bohemia, Silverhill, St Helens and Old London Road; 1945 – Circular via Bohemia, Silverhill, St Helens and Old London Road: 1957 – became T2 renumbered post Maidstone & District rebranding
3	1932 – Hollington to Alexandra Park via London Road; 1945 – Silverhill to Ore via London Road (some extended to St Helens); 1946 – no longer operated
4	1932 – Hollington to Fish Market via Bohemia; 1945 – not operated
5	1932 – Ore to Cooden via Mount Pleasant; 1945 – Alexandra Park to Cooden via Memorial; 1949 – renumbered service 8; 1957 – became T8 renumbered post Maidstone & District rebranding
6	1932 – Langham to West Marina; 1945 – Hollington to Ore via Bohemia Road, Memorial and Mount Pleasant; 1957 – became T6 renumbered post Maidstone & District rebranding
7	1932 – St Helens to Bexhill Metropole via Mount Pleasant; 1945 – not operated
8	1932 – Silverhill to West Marina (summer only); 1945 – not operated
9	1932 – Hastings station to Ore via Clive Vale; 1945 – Hollington to Ore via Bohemia Road, Memorial and Clive Vale (some extended to St Helens); 1946 – no longer operated
10	1932 – Hastings station to Ore via Fish Market and Old London Road; 1945 – not operated
11	1932 – Hollington to Ore via London Road and Clive Vale; 1945 – Hollington to Ore via London Road and Clive Vale; 1957 – became T11 renumbered post Maidstone & District rebranding
12	1932 – Hollington to Mount Pleasant via London Road and Laton Road 1940 – Hollington to Langham via Bohemia Road, Queens Road and Laton Road 1945 – not operated

Two views taken on 25 May 1958, almost exactly a year before the system was abandoned, sees (above) 1947-built Sunbeam W No 41, which was sold to Walsall Corporation in 1959, on High Street at its junction with Swan Terrace with a service on route 11 towards Hollington and (below) one of the older generation of double-deck trolleybuses – AEC 661T No 5 of 1940 heading for Silverhill – at the Fish Market. *C. Carter/Online Transport Archive (both)*

LONDON

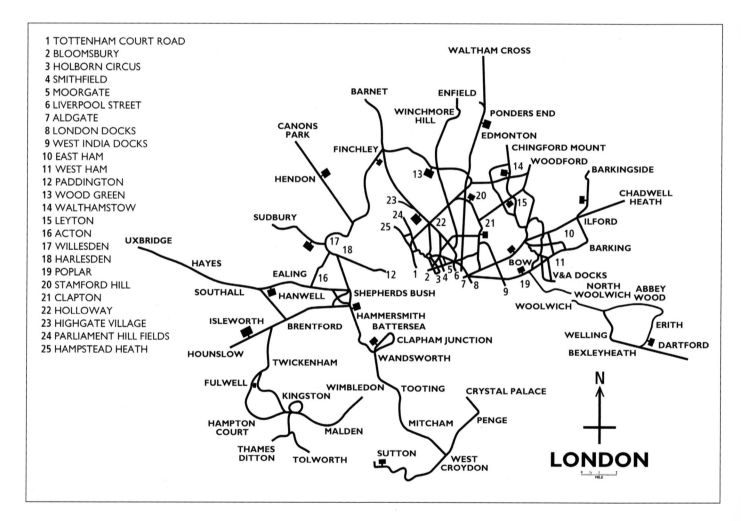

1 TOTTENHAM COURT ROAD
2 BLOOMSBURY
3 HOLBORN CIRCUS
4 SMITHFIELD
5 MOORGATE
6 LIVERPOOL STREET
7 ALDGATE
8 LONDON DOCKS
9 WEST INDIA DOCKS
10 EAST HAM
11 WEST HAM
12 PADDINGTON
13 WOOD GREEN
14 WALTHAMSTOW
15 LEYTON
16 ACTON
17 WILLESDEN
18 HARLESDEN
19 POPLAR
20 STAMFORD HILL
21 CLAPTON
22 HOLLOWAY
23 HIGHGATE VILLAGE
24 PARLIAMENT HILL FIELDS
25 HAMPSTEAD HEATH

Although it was not until 1931 that trolleybuses made their first appearance in public service in London, the history of this form of transport in the metropolis stretches back more than two decades before that date.

The first trolleybus to be built and operated in the British Isles was one supplied through the Railless Electric Traction Co Ltd and demonstrated at the MET's Hendon depot to representatives attending the Municipal Tramways Association annual conference between 25 and 29 September 1909 and again members of Middlesex County Council's Light Railways and Tramways Committee on 19 October 1909. Although there were plans for a route, these came to nothing and the experimental overhead was removed in 1911. The Hendon demonstration was the first of a number of experiments in the London area. The next – during September 1912 – saw the demonstration of a

The first trolleybus to operate in London – indeed the first built in Britain – was an experimental vehicle produced for the Metropolitan Electric Tramways by the Railless Electric Traction Co in 1909. Fitted with a 24-seat body supplied by Milnes Voss, the trolleybus was demonstrated at Hendon depot for the first time on 25 September 1909. The vehicle – as illustrated here – carried a route board promoting a service from Golders Green to Hendon. This had previously been promoted as a possible tram route but had been progressed and, following the demonstration of the new trolleybus, negotiations commenced with Hendon UDC over the possible introduction of a trolleybus route. These, however, did not proceed smoothly and, although the UDC gave approval, the conditions demanded were too onerous for the company to accept. The possibility of establishing a trolleybus service was eventually thwarted by the introduction of a London General bus service between Hendon and Golders Green in March 1911. This was not quite the end for the MET's aspirations to operate trolleybuses; a further service was proposed in 1913 for which powers were obtained. Unfortunately, the First World War intervened and, although the powers were renewed, the service was never introduced. *London Transport/D.W.K. Jones Collection/Online Transport Archive*

Cedes-Stoll trolleybus in West Ham. The next saw overhead erected, on behalf of LUT, in Wimbledon during 1921 with trial operation of a trolleybus commencing in January 1922; it is possible that more than one trolleybus was demonstrated before the overhead was removed and at least one other vehicle – later Leeds No 513 – was also demonstrated at Fulwell depot. There was sufficient interest for a number of proposers to seek powers but, whilst a number received parliamentary approval, none were constructed.

This was to change following the passage of the London United Tramways Act 1930, which received the Royal Assent on 1 August 1930. The LUT's financial position had deteriorated considerably since the end of the Second World War and it faced a number of threats. As a company-owned undertaking it was under the threat of being taken over by the local authorities pursuant to the terms of the 1870 Tramways Act. Its infrastructure and vehicles were increased life-expired and requiring investment; investment that was difficult to justify if the entire undertaking was to be taken over. In an era before public transport was regulated there was also the threat from numerous private bus operators competing for the traffic.

In terms of determining the future, the most influential figure was Christopher John Spencer; as general manager at Bradford he had overseen the introduction of trolleybuses to that system and he moved to London in 1918, where he managed not only the LUT but also the MET and the South Met. Although he was instrumental in the development of the 'Feltham' type of tram, which placated the local authorities involved with both the LUT and MET, he was also keen to see the trolleybus developed. He recognised that the future for the tram was uncertain but that the trolleybus made use of much of the electrical infrastructure associated with the trams, infrastructure that was both capital intensive and also still capable of years of additional operation.

During 1912, whilst a tramway conference was being held at Stratford, the opportunity was taken to demonstrate a Cedes-Stoll trolleybus. The demonstration vehicle is seen here in Greengate Street, Plaistow, alongside West Ham Corporation tram No 114; the latter was one of a batch of twelve open-balcony cars supplied by Hurst Nelson in 1911. *Tramway & Railway World/Barry Cross Collection/Online Transport Archive*

On 1 May 1930, the directors of London United Tramways approved the hiring of a double-deck trolleybus from AERC for demonstration purposes at Fulwell depot. The vehicle – illustrated here – was the first AEC 663T to be constructed; the chassis was based on the successful AEC Renown bus chassis with electrical equipment supplied by English Electric (the two companies had set up a joint marketing agreement for the production of trolleybuses during March 1930). The body was built by English Electric and the vehicle initially carried the trade plates 471H. It was subsequently to be registered HX1460. Following its demonstration in London on 1 October 1930, it was subsequently used in Nottingham. Rebuilt with a new half-cab English Electric body, the vehicle was displayed at the 1931 Commercial Motor Show. *D.W.K. Jones Collection/Online Transport Archive*

Work proceeded on the conversion of the initial routes and three demonstrators were shown at Fulwell depot whilst, contemporaneously, the construction of the first batch of 'Diddlers' was in hand. On 16 May 1931, London's first trolleybuses were officially introduced to the 2½-mile section from Twickenham to Teddington; between then and 2 September the original LUT network was progressively opened. The LUT constructed two extensions; the first of these in Wimbledon opened on 15 December 1932 with the second – authorised by the London United (Trolley Vehicles) Provisional Order Act 1932, which gained the Royal Assent on 12 July 1932 – in Tolworth following on 20 September 1933. By that date, however, London's trolleybuses were under new management, following the creation on 1 July 1933 of the London Passenger Transport Board.

The LPTB inherited a large tramway network from a disparate number of operators; the largest of these was the erstwhile London County Council but, apart from the three companies, there were also a number of municipal operators, such as West Ham and Ilford. A number of services had been jointly run but now, for the first time, they came under single ownership. The future of the system was inevitably under consideration and, with Spencer still retaining a significant role within the new organisation, the

The last of the trolleybuses ordered pre-war by the LPTB were delivered during 1941. In order to supplement the existing fleet and to replace the significant number of vehicles seriously damaged or destroyed as a result of enemy action, the LPTB was loaned eighteen Bournemouth vehicles from 1940 until 1941 or 1942 and received three batches of trolleybuses – Nos 1722-64 – that had been diverted from orders made by South African operators. These vehicles were all 8ft 0in wide – the first of this width to operate in the metropolis (and wider than permitted by the Ministry of Transport at the time). Apart from the vehicles completely destroyed as a result of the Blitz and other enemy action, a further sixty-one were rebodied, sixteen by Weymann during 1941 and 1942 with the other forty-five being so treated by East Lancs between 1945 and 1948 or by NCB during 1946. The vehicles rebodied operated thereafter with a suffix after their fleet number.

The Second World War had prevented the completion of the LPTB's tramway conversion programme. A significant network of lines, inherited from the LCC or Croydon Council, remained operational. In early 1946 a report was issued which commented on 'The urgent necessity of replacing trams in South London with a more modern and attractive form of transport.' On 15 November 1946, a later statement made it clear that the 'more modern and attractive form of transport' was to be the motorbus rather than the trolleybus. However, initially, the priority was to restore a war-battered system rather than tram replacement; indeed, over the next few years some £1 million was spent refurbishing the surviving tram network with, for example, a number of trams having their bodywork strengthened and sections of life-expired track being replaced.

The policies of the post-war Labour government saw the Nationalisation of much of Britain's core industries, including transport and the LPTB was not to escape this. Following the passage of the Transport Act 1947, which received the Royal Assent on 6 August 1947, the LPTB was dissolved and replaced by a new body – the nationalised

Following the withdrawal of the bulk of the 'Diddlers' during 1948 and 1949, the redundant vehicles were disposed of for scrap. A significant number were sold to George Cohen & Son Ltd, being dismantled by the contractor at Poplar depot as recorded in this view of work in progress. Four – Nos 47, 51, 56 and 57 – were scrapped by the LTE itself at Fulwell. *Geoffrey Ashwell/ Online Transport Archive*

London Transport Executive – on 1 January 1948. For the next two years it was to be very much business as before, although the number of operational tramcars gradually declined, there were no route conversions and – during 1948 and 1949 – the LTE took delivery of the first of the new 8ft 0in wide 'Q1' class, Nos 1765-1841. The arrival of these vehicles permitted the withdrawal of all of the trolleybuses inherited in 1933 from the LUT; one of the 'Diddlers' was preserved – the first London trolleybus secured for posterity.

On 5 July 1950 Lord Latham, chairman of the LTE, announced the long-expected programme for tramway replacement. Costing £10 million, the plan anticipated nine stages over a three-year period; in reality, there were eight stages and the programme was completed within two years. The first stage of the conversion programme occurred over the weekend of 30 September / 1 October 1950. In addition to five all-day tram services and two night services, this conversion also resulted in the abandonment of trolleybus service No 612 from Mitcham to Battersea as the route was integrated into the replacement motorbus services introduced on 1 October 1950. There was as yet no policy of wholesale policy for trolleybus conversion and, in 1952, the LTE took delivery of a further batch of fifty 'Q1s'; these were, however, destined to be the last new trolleybuses to be acquired by the LTE.

The unique Class X1 (or A3) No 61 is pictured in Fulwell depot on 13 July 1952; by this date the vehicle had been withdrawn from passenger service, but it was not sold for scrap until February 1954. An AEC 691T fitted with a body built by London General at Chiswick, No 61 was the last new trolleybus acquired by LUT and the first to feature a full front. It was also equipped with a central door – the only trolleybus in London so fitted – and its longer bodywork could accommodate seventy-four seated passengers. For a period from March 1945 it was modified to operate as a Pay as You Board vehicle on route 604 but was to finish its career working on the 657. For a brief period following withdrawal from service in September 1951 it was used a training vehicle based at Fulwell. *John Meredith/Online Transport Archive*

The first trolleybuses acquired by the LPTB were Nos 62 and 63 that were prototype vehicles produced by AEC and fitted with Metro-Cammell (No 62) or English Electric (No 63) bodywork. No 62 – pictured here at Manor House towards the end of its life when it had been transferred to Holloway depot following the delivery the first batch of 'Q1s' – was based on the AEC 663T three-axle chassis and was originally allocated to Fulwell. Designated Class X2, No 62 was new in July 1934 and was withdrawn in October 1952. *J. Joyce Collection/Online Transport Archive*

The last trams operated in July 1952 and attention turned to the future of the trolleybus network. On 28 April 1954, it was announced that, with the approval of the British Transport Commission, the trolleybus network was to be replaced by motorbuses – in particular by the new Routemaster – with some 1,600 required to replace the trolleybus fleet. The reasons given were similar to those put forward elsewhere. The report highlighted the following: buses were more mobile, more flexible (making extensions easier to introduce), less prone to cause delays through dewirements or power cuts, more easily diverted (for example to serve major sporting events) and more adaptable. The proposed changeover was again to be undertaken in stages with the final stage – based on Fulwell and Isleworth depots – covering the relatively self-contained network inherited from the LUT. It was anticipated that, given the relatively new 'Q1s', this the final conversion would take place when the batch was life-expired.

The first phase of the conversion programme – on 4 March 1959 – resulted in the withdrawal of the isolated services based on Bexleyheath along with the route from Sutton to Crystal Palace. Between then and 3 January 1962 there were to be a further twelve stages in the programme – on 15 April 1959, 19 August 1959, 11 November 1959, 3 February 1960, 27 April 1960, 20 July 1960, 9 November 1960, 1 February 1961, 26 April 1961, 19 July 1961, 8 November 1961 and 3 January 1962 – that saw the trolleybus eliminated from most of its traditional haunts. These conversions resulted in the trolleybus network being cut back to the system inherited in 1933 plus services 657 and 667.

In theory, these services were to have survived through until the point at which the post-war trolleybuses had 'completed their full life' as outlined in the 1954 plan. However, the decision to withdraw the 'Q1s' during the period from November 1960 through to April 1961 and sell all bar two of them to Spanish operators for re-use meant that this policy was no longer valid and, as a result, the final stage of London's trolleybus-to-motorbus policy took place on 9 May 1962. Alongside the sole surviving 'Diddler', which was brought out of retirement for the occasion, 'L3' No 1521 was decorated at Fulwell depot to act as the official last trolleybus. The conversion of the ex-LUT routes resulted in the final demise of what had been, at one stage, the world's largest trolleybus operators.

Of the London fleet, apart from No 1 and No 1521 (eventually), a further six examples – Nos 260. 796, 1201, 1253, 1348 and 1768 – were secured for preservation whilst a second 'Q1', No 1812, was repatriated from Spain following withdrawal there. A further four examples of the type – modified for use in Spain – survive there.

Class X3 No 63 was – famously – the only two-axle trolleybus to be operated in London and was based on the AEC 661T chassis. Also allocated to Fulwell when new in August 1934, it is pictured here on route 604 at Hampton Court. Both Nos 62 and 63 were regularly used on the 604 and 605 before the arrival of the first 'Q1s'; No 63 was to spend its last years based at Hounslow for use primarily on route 657. No 63 was withdrawn in June 1952; it and No 62 were sold for scrap in February 1954. *J. Joyce Collection/Online Transport Archive*

Above: **Recorded at** the Wimbledon Stadium terminus on Plough Lane during a Southern Counties Touring Society special is 'B1' No 73 on 30 September 1951. The first significant delivery of trolleybuses after the creation of the LPTB in July 1933 was represented by the thirty examples of Class B1 that were delivered during 1935 and 1936; Nos 64-93 were Leyland TTB2s fitted with BRCW sixty-seat bodywork; all were rebuilt at Fulwell in the late 1930s. This and the subsequent 'B2' class with their short wheelbases were designed for routes that featured hilly sections, narrow streets, etc. *John Meredith/Online Transport Archive*

Opposite above: **All thirty** of the 'B1' class were allocated to Sutton depot for use on the 654 for their entire operational life and it is at Crystal Palace that this view of No 87 was recorded. The 'B1' class – unlike the 'B2' type – was equipped with coasting and run back brakes to prevent the vehicles running back out of control when operating on Anerley Hill at Crystal Palace. The first of the batch was withdrawn in 1955, but the bulk survived until the conversion of route 654 in March 1959. *Marcus Eavis/Online Transport Archive*

Opposite below: **Alongside the** 'B1s' were the similarly-chassised Class B2; the major difference between the two types was that the 'B2s' were fitted with Brush-built sixty-seat bodies. The batch – Nos 94-131 – all entered service between October and December 1935 and, again like, the 'B1s' all were rebuilt but at Charlton (rather than Fulwell) during the late 1930s. No 99 was destroyed as a result of enemy action in Bexleyheath during June 1944 and a number of others were severely damaged on other occasions and rebuilt. Apart from No 99, the first withdrawal occurred in December 1951 and all had been withdrawn by the end of January 1953 with the exception of the quartet rebuilt by Weymann and Northern Coachbuilders, which were withdrawn between July 1958 and March 1959. Here two of the types – Nos 113 and 125 – are pictured at the South End Green, Hampstead, terminus on 14 April 1952 towards the end of their lives; they were withdrawn in June 1952 and May 1952 respectively. *John Meredith/Online Transport Archive*

Above: **A total** of sixty-two Class C1s – Nos 132-83 – were delivered between September and November 1935 and here No 142, the first of the Metro-Cammell-bodied examples, is pictured at the AEC works at Southall in October 1935 when newly delivered. As illustrated, the class, with the exception on No 183, was fitted with deep red-painted mudguards when new; these were modified during the Second World War. All were AEC 664Ts; Nos 132-41 were fitted with seventy-seat bodywork supplied by Weymann whilst the remainder had similar bodies produced by Metro-Cammell. When new the class was allocated to Fulwell and Hounslow depots with a handful being briefly based at Bexleyheath. Following the delivery of the 'Q1s' the type was transferred to serve routes in north London, all being withdrawn between March and June 1955. Five of the class – including No 142 – were sold in 1956 to Georgetown Municipal Transport in Malaya, where they were to survive until withdrawal in November 1959. *D.W.K. Jones Collection/Online Transport Archive*

Opposite above: **Pictured at** Hendon depot prior to the conversion of 5 July 1936 which involved the replacement of tram routes 66 and 68 as well as existing trolleybus service 660 into the new trolleybus route 666, one of the 100-strong 'C2' class of AEC 664Ts fitted with Metro-Cammell seventy-seat bodywork – No 223 – is seen at Hendon depot alongside ex-MET Class C2 Nos 2483 and 2489, which were, by this date, approaching the end of their thirty-year career. When new the 'C2', delivered between March and August 1936, were allocated to Acton, Finchley, Hendon and Stonebridge Park and were largely to remain there until withdrawal. All were withdrawn between March 1955 and November 1959, with No 260 being preserved following withdrawal in August 1959. Displayed for a period at the Museum of British Transport at Clapham, No 260 led a somewhat charmed life as, in July 1962 it was sold to George Cohen for scrap before being privately purchased for preservation. *D.W.K. Jones/National Tramway Museum*

Opposite below: **On 13 August** 1955, Class C3 No 323 is seen on Chichele Road, Cricklewood, whilst operating a route 664 service to Edgware. The hundred-strong 'C3' type – Nos 284-323 – were AEC 664Ts fitted with BRCW seventy-seat bodywork. Of these, the first fifty, including No 323 as illustrated, were fitted with metal spats, which were easily removable if required, covering the upper half of the rear wheels; the spats were to be retained throughout their operational life. The remainder had black mudguards, but these were modified before the war. The type entered service between April 1936 and December 1936, being initially allocated to Acton, Hendon, Finchley and Stonebridge Park for use on routes 645, 660, 662, 664 and 666. All were withdrawn between March 1955 and November 1959. *John Meredith/Online Transport Archive*

Above: **In January** 1945 No 378 was damaged by enemy action at Walthamstow depot. As a result, it was rebuilt for use in the experimental 'Pay as you Board' service alongside No 61. The work involved modifying its rear platform to accommodate a conductor's cash desk and the installation of power-operated platform doors. The resulting conversion is seen here outside Fulwell depot, where Nos 61 and 378 were based for the experimental service on route 604. The experiment ran from December 1945 through to March 1946 and No 378 was further modified, losing its platform doors. *D.W.K. Jones Collection/Online Transport Archive*

Opposite above: **On 2 September** 1953 Class D2 No 449 is seen on Tamworth Road, West Croydon, awaiting departure with a service on route 630. A total of ninety-nine – No 385-483 – of the 'D2' class were delivered between September 1936 and April 1937 and were initially allocated to Hanwell and Acton but were transferred to Hammersmith for use on routes 626, 628 and 630 following the delivery of the 'F1s'. Eight were destroyed during the Second World War and a number of others sustained damage that required rebuilding. Withdrawal post-war commenced in February 1956 and the last succumbed in April 1959; No 449 was one of those that remained active until that last month. *Gerald Druce/Online Transport Archive*

Opposite below: **Class B1** No 492 is seen at the South End Green, Hampstead, terminus of route 639 prior to heading south to Moorgate on 14 April 1952. In September 1936, a further ten 'B' type Leylands fitted with BRCW sixty-seat bodywork were delivered; Class B3 Nos 484-88 and Class B1 Nos 489-93 were designed to provide reserves for the earlier sixty-seat vehicles. The five 'B3s' were modified at Charlton during 1938 whilst the 'B1s' underwent work contemporaneously at Fulwell. The five 'B1s' were allocated to Holloway for the bulk of their careers, but latterly spent some time at Sutton or briefly, in one case, at Hammersmith. The five 'B1s' were all withdrawn between June 1957 and March 1959. *John Meredith/Online Transport Archive*

Above: On 23 September 1950, Class D3 No 503 is recorded leaving Jews Row, Wandsworth, with a peak hour working to West Croydon. The 'D' type represented 160 Leyland LPTB70s split into three classes each with seventy-seat bodywork delivered between April 1936 and November 1937: Class D1 No 384 was unique in being bodied by Leyland, Class D2 Nos 385-483 were bodied by Metro-Cammell whilst Class D3 Nos 494-553 had bodies supplied by BRCW. The sixty 'D3's were initially allocated to Hammersmith (for use on services 626, 628 and 630) and Wandsworth (for route 612 with duties on the 630 being added in 1944). Following the conversion on route 612 on 30 September 1950, the Wandsworth-allocated 'D3s were transferred to Walthamstow. A number subsequently saw service from Highgate and Bexleyheath. The 'D3s' were withdrawn between January 1953 and April 1959. *John Meredith/Online Transport Archive*

Opposite above: On 18 July 1959, Class E1 No 558 stands at Edgware awaiting departure with a service on route 666 towards Hammersmith as Class C3 No 314 overtakes with a service on route 645 towards Barnet. The fifty-strong 'E1' class – Nos 554-603 – was delivered between May and October 1937. The type was initially allocated to Ilford, Walthamstow and West Ham but a number – including No 558 – were transferred to Stonebridge in 1955 for use on services such as the 666. The type was withdrawn between May 1955 and February 1960; by the date that No 558 was recorded here, it was approaching the end of its operational life as it was withdrawn the following month. *Gerald Druce/Online Transport Archive*

Opposite below: On 9 May 1959, Class E2 No 617 is pictured at the North Woolwich terminus of route 669; this was one of four services converted to bus operation on 2 February 1960. The 'E2' class of AEC 664Ts bodied by Weymann was twenty-five strong and was delivered during April to June 1937. All were allocated to West Ham for use on services 669, 685, 689 and 690; one of the batch – No 621 – was rebodied following damage during the Second World War and spent a period allocated to Fulwell – the only occasion on which an 'E2' was based anyway other than West Ham; others rebodied post-war as a result of enemy action were Nos 623, 626 and 629. All of the 'E2s' were withdrawn between November 1956 and February 1960 with the exception of No 622. This survived a further three months to enable to become the last trolleybus to operate from West Ham depot; it had carried a commemorative plaque noting that it had been the first trolleybus to operate from West Ham depot. *John Meredith/Online Transport Archive*

Above: **Trolleybuses of** two generations await departure from the Uxbridge terminus of route 607. On the left is Class F1 No 717 whilst on the right is 'Q1' No 1852. The former was one of a hundred – Nos 654-753 – Leylands fitted with Leyland seventy-seat bodywork that entered service between February and December 1937. All were initially allocated to Hanwell for operation on routes 607, 655 and 666 and largely remained based there for their entire career although, in later years, a number were to be transferred to other depots. The final survivors of the type – including No 717 – were all withdrawn in November 1960. No 1852 was one of the fifty 'Q1s' delivered during 1952. Withdrawn in February 1961, it was exported to Spain where it entered service in San Sebastian – one of twenty-five that went to that operator. *Julian Thompson/Online Transport Archive*

Opposite above: **On 29 May** 1950 'F1' class No 750 is seen at the Ravensbury Arms, Mitcham Common, with a special Bank Holiday special that originated from Hanwell depot. No 750 was amongst the earliest of the type to be withdrawn, being taken out of service in February 1960. *John Meredith/Online Transport Archive*

Opposite below: **No 754** – the unique Class X4 – is seen here inside its home depot of Finchley, where it was based for its entire operational career, alongside 'C3' No 328. No 754 was the only trolleybus to be constructed by London Transport itself and was also the first chassisless vehicle to enter service. In additional to the experimental nature of the vehicle's construction, No 754 was also equipped with a front exit fitted with folding doors as part of an operational experiment. This modification resulted in the seating capacity being slightly reduced. The exit was locked out of use during the vehicle's later years. New in April 1937, No 754 was primarily used on Finchley-based routes Nos 521, 609 and 621. It was withdrawn in March 1955. *Harry Luff/Online Transport Archive*

Above: Class H1 No 841 overtakes Country Area No RT4791, which was new in September 1954, at the Enfield Town terminus with a service on route 629 during 1958. The 150-strong 'H1' class was delivered between November 1937 to July 1938 and were Leyland LPTB70s fitted with Metro-Cammell seventy-seat bodies. The vehicles were initially allocated to Holloway, Wood Green, Walthamstow and Edmonton depots for the routes converted that year. Three of the type were withdrawn and a number of others were rebuilt due to war damage. Apart from the trio withdrawn during the war, the remainder were all withdrawn between September 1955 and February 1961; No 841 was a relatively early casualty, succumbing in April 1959 following the conversion of routes 555, 581 and 677. Route 629 was converted to bus operation on 26 April 1961. One of the 'H1' class – No 796 – survives in preservation. *Marcus Eavis/Online Transport Archive*

Opposite above: Class J1 No 920 pauses at a zebra crossing as it heads along Farringdon Street during 1958 with a service on route 621 towards North Finchley. A total of forty-eight AEC 664Ts fitted with Weymann seventy-seat bodywork – Nos 905-52 – were delivered between November 1937 and April 1938. The class was initially allocated to Finchley for use on routes 521, 621 and 651; the type was associated with Finchley for the bulk of the vehicles' careers although during 1959 and 1960 some were reallocated to Highgate and Walthamstow. Withdrawal of the type commenced in July 1958 and all had been taken out of service by the end of April 1960. *Marcus Eavis/Online Transport Archive*

Opposite below: In February 1938, the LPTB took delivery of No 953; this was a pre-production prototype of the later 'M1' class designed to illustrate concepts of integral construction and utilised the manufacturer's patented lightweight chassis frame allied to a Weymann seventy-seat body. When new, No 953 was allocated to West Ham but was destined for a relatively short operational life, being destroyed by fire in late 1943. It is pictured here at West Ham depot. *London Transport/John Meredith Collection/Online Transport Archive*

Above: **Pictured at** the North Finchley terminus of route 521 is No 965; this was one of the seventy-five-strong 'J2' class that were delivered between February and June 1938. Four of the type suffered damage during the Second World War and were subsequently rebuilt. They were withdrawn between July 1958 and April 1960. *Harry Luff/Online Transport Archive*

Opposite above: **No 1048,** seen here turning at the Highgate Village terminus of route 611 prior to heading back to Moorgate in 1960, was one of the Class J3. This batch comprise twenty-five AEC 664Ts fitted with BRCW bodywork – Nos 1030-54 – that were delivered between August and October 1938. The only difference between this type and the outwardly similar Class J2 was that the 'J3s' were equipped with coasting and run-back brakes that were essential, under police regulations, for operation on Highgate Hill. The 611 was the only service that traversed the section – there were plans, never completed, to divert the 517 and 617 – and were based at Holloway for that route, although prior to the 611's conversion on 10 December 1939, they were used on other services. The 611 was converted to bus operation on 20 July 1960 and, with the exception of No 1054, which survived until November 1960, all had been withdrawn by the end of January 1961. *Marcus Eavis/Online Transport Archive*

Opposite below: **The first** of the 150-strong 'K1' class – No 1055 – is seen turning right from Kentish Town Road into Fortess Road with a service on route 639. Nos 1055-154/255-304 were delivered between September 1938 and June 1939 and were initially allocated to various north and east London depots but in later years a number were transferred to Fulwell, Hammersmith, Hanwell, Isleworth and Wood Green. Route 639 duties were allocated to Holloway (Highgate) depot, which lost its allocation on 25 April 1961, three months after the conversion of the 639. *Julian Thompson/Online Transport Archive*

Above: A total of 150 Class K2s – Nos 1155-254/305-354 – were delivered between September 1938 and June 1939. The only difference effectively between the class and the contemporary 'K1' was that the latter had Metrovick control equipment whilst the 'K2s' had equipment supplied by English Electric. During their careers, the 'K' types operated from a number of depots – including Edmonton, Hackney (for use on routes including the 581 on which No 1311 is pictured at Whipps Cross during 1959) and Holloway – as well as latterly at Hanwell. The first 'K2' to be withdrawn was one of those rebuilt as a result of wartime damage – No 1244A – in July 1957 and the remainder were withdrawn in early November 1961. *Marcus Eavis/Online Transport Archive*

Opposite above: Here 'K2' No 1201 – which was to be eventually preserved (one of two to survive, the other being No 1253 which now forms part of the London Transport Museum collection) – is seen at the Liverpool Street terminus on Bishopsgate with a service on route 649A on 16 July 1961. A number of the 'K1s' were transferred in 1961 from their traditional haunts – such as Stamford Hill (where No 1201 was allocated when pictured) – to Isleworth for use on the 657 following the sale of the 'Q1s'. The first 'K1' to be withdrawn was No 1257 in July 1958 but a significant number were still in service when the system was finally converted. After No 1201's withdrawal it was sold to Welton Auto Services of Shepherds Bush for use as an office; it was secured for preservation in August 1968. *John Meredith/Online Transport Archive*

Opposite below: The sole representative of Class X5 was No 1379 – seen here working route 653 at Aldgate – which was an AEC fitted with a Metro-Cammell sixty-eight-seat body that was new in June 1936. The vehicle was designed as the prototype for the operation of trolleybuses through the Kingsway Subway and thus had a number of detailed differences from the 'L3' class. One of these, clearly visible in the photograph, was the provision of an offside rear doorway with folding doors; this was to facilitate the use of the central island platforms at those stops on the subway. The vehicle was also provided with coasting and run back brakes for use on the northern – Southampton Row – ramp to enter the subway. In the event, war and the decision eventually to replace the subway trams by buses resulted in no further modified vehicles. Although passenger operation through the subway by trolleybus was never introduced, No 1379 was used on two test trips through the subway during August 1939; the timing could not have been much worse! As a non-standard vehicle, No 1379 was a relatively early casualty, being withdrawn in March 1955. *Geoffrey Ashwell/Online Transport Archive*

Above: Pictured at the Moorgate terminus on 18 July 1959 are Class L1 No 1362 and Class 'J1' No 910. The 'L1' class represented the first of the chassisless types to be produced, being delivered between March and May 1939. Allocated to Holloway when new, the type never migrated from that depot during their operational life. One of the type – No 1365 – was destroyed by fire in March 1945 but the remainder survived until withdrawal between October 1959 and January 1961. *Gerald Druce/Online Transport Archive*

Opposite above: **During the** spring of 1962, Class L3 No 1395 is pictured picking up passengers with a service on route 601 in Kingston. A total of 150 of the type – AEC chassisless with Metro-Cammell 70-seat bodywork – were delivered between July 1939 and May 1940. The initial vehicles in the batch were allocated when new to Holloway but subsequent deliveries were based at Poplar and West Ham in connection with the conversion of the Commercial Road tram routes. In February 1961, most of the Holloway-allocated 'L3s' were transferred to Fulwell to permit the transfer of the 'Q1s' to Spain. Two vehicles were destroyed during the war – Nos 1387 and 1492 – with No 1385 being damaged but rebuilt. Although the withdrawal of the type began in May 1959, a significant number remained operational through until the final conversion of the system in May 1962. No 1521 was destined to act as London's official last trolleybus; it and No 1348 both survive in preservation, the latter at Sandtoft. *Marcus Eavis/Online Transport Archive*

Opposite below: **Class M1** No 1552 leads an impressive line up of trolleybuses as it awaits departure from Moorgate with a service to Hampstead Heath on route 639 during 1960. The 25 members of the class – Nos 1530-554 – were AEC chassisless fitted with Weymann seventy-seat bodywork and were delivered between October to December 1939. The first of the batch were initially allocated to Bow, with later examples, which were used for the conversion of the Commercial Road tram routes, being based at West Ham. Two of the type – Nos 1543 and 1545 – were seriously damaged during the war and were rebodied on conventional AEC 664T chassis in 1948. In the early 1950s those allocated to Bow were transferred to Highgate and the 1960/61 conversions saw a number transferred to Highgate and Finchley. The last of the type were withdrawn in November 1961. *Marcus Eavis/Online Transport Archive*

Above: **Class N1** No 1567 stands outside Lea Bridge depot alongside RT282 during 1959. The 'N1' and 'N2' classes represented the last AEC 664Ts delivered to the LPTB; the former also represented the last trolleybuses to be bodied by BRCW for the LPTB. Two of the 'N1s' suffered war damage and were subsequently rebuilt. The 'N1s', delivered between June and December 1939, were initially allocated to Bow for use on routes 661 and 663 and remained largely allocated there until the conversion of the two routes on 19 August 1959; thereafter they were dispersed to a number of other depots. Lea Bridge depot, which had had its first allocation of trolleybuses on 11 June 1939, was closed to trolleybuses on 14 April 1959. The first 'N1' to be withdrawn was No 1565A – one of the two rebuilt following war damage – in March 1958, with the remainder succumbing between September 1959 and January 1962. *Marcus Eavis/Online Transport Archive*

Opposite above: **On 26 January** 1961 Class N2 No 1666 and Class L3 No 1424 are seen on Caledonian Road, King's Cross, on routes 617 and 517 respectively; by this date, both services were approaching the end as they were converted to bus operation six days later. Both of the trolleybuses illustrated were to survive for longer, however, being withdrawn in January 1962 and November 1961 respectively. No 1666 was one of the twenty-five-strong 'N2' class that was delivered between June and December 1940, being allocated to Bow and Poplar depots when new. The type's later career saw them operating from Finchley, Highgate, Walthamstow and West Ham depots but latterly the vast majority were based at Stonebridge Park. The first casualty was No 1662, which was destroyed by fire at Charlton Works in November 1956, with the remainder being withdrawn between September 1959 and January 1962. *John Meredith/Online Transport Archive*

Opposite below: **The future** No 1671 was built in February 1939 as a demonstrator by Leyland and was to enter service with the LPTB in September 1939; classified 'X7' by the board, the vehicle was chassisless with a body accommodating seventy seated passengers. The unusual arrangement – with twin steering axles at the front – was designed to reduce tyre scrub on corners; this was a problem with the rigid two axles of the conventional three-axle design and could cause damage to the road surface. Based at Fulwell initially and largely used on route 667, the vehicle was transferred to transferred to Hanwell after the 'Q1' started to be received and spent much of its later career on routes 607 and 655. As another non-standard type, No 1671 was an early casualty, being withdrawn in May 1955. *Geoffrey Ashwell/Online Transport Archive*

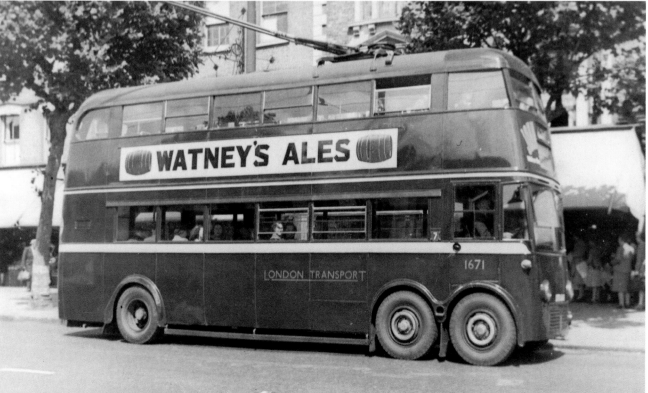

Above: **Pictured heading** past Barking station with a service on route 691 is 'SA2' No 1739. Like all of the trolleybuses originally destined for South Africa, the 'SA1s' were delivered with front doors; those on the 'SA1s' and 'SA2s' were designed to slide and those on the 'SA3s' to fold but all were modified after delivery to London to have the doorways panelled over. Other facets that distinguished these from more native vehicles were partially tinted windows and the fact that all the windows were drop opening (although the LPTB locked half the latter permanently shut). All the 'SA2s' were withdrawn in August 1959. *Julian Thompson/Online Transport Archive*

Right: **Pictured on** the loop at the Chadwell Heath terminus of route 693 is 'SA2' No 1738. Like the 'SA1' class, Nos 1734-46 had originally been ordered by Durban in South Africa. The thirteen were delivered to the LPTB between February and July 1942. All were allocated to Ilford for their entire operational life, with all being withdrawn during August 1959 following the conversion of the 693 on the 19th of that month. *Harry Luff/Online Transport Archive*

Delivered between January 1948 and January 1953, the 127 members of the 'Q1' class represented the last new trolleybuses acquired by London Transport as well as the only vehicles the system acquired post-war. The initial batch of seventy-seven were all in service by March 1949 with the remainder all being delivered during 1952/53. The first batch was allocated to Fulwell, where their arrival permitted the withdrawal of a number of older vehicles – most notably the ex-LUT 'Diddlers' – with the 1952 examples being allocated initially to both Fulwell and Isleworth (between 1953 and 1960 about twenty were allocated to Hanwell depot). All were BUT 9641Ts fitted with Metro-Cammell 8ft 0in wide bodies accommodating seventy seated passengers. Initially the trolleybus conversion plan anticipated the retention of the post-war vehicles to operate the original LUT network 'for the time being' whilst their vehicles 'completed their full life'. In the event, the decision to sell the vehicles to a number of Spanish operators resulted in their premature withdrawal. No 1808, which had been new in July 1948 and is seen here outside the Burton shop on King Street, Hammersmith, was withdrawn as a result in February 1961. It was one of the type that was to see further service at Coruna in Spain. Of the 127, 125 travelled to Spain; of the remaining two, No 1768, was preserved whilst No 1841 was scrapped in the UK with the motors passing to Imperial College. Subsequently a second example – No 1812 – was repatriated from Spain, where it had operated in Santander – for preservation and restoration. *Julian Thompson/Online Transport Archive*

Right: **It is** 4 November 1956 and evidence of the withdrawal of London's trolleybuses is evident in this view of the scrapyard at Stratford-upon-Avon of the dealer Bird. Of the trolleybuses visible, only one – 'C2' class No 247 – is identifiable. This vehicle was withdrawn during March 1955 and made its final journey to the scrapyard in April the following year. *Neil Davenport/Online Transport Archive*

Opposite above: **As part** of the events to mark the final conversion of the London system, the only surviving 'Diddler – the preserved No 1 – was temporarily brought out of store to operate a ceremonial final run over the routes that it had first been introduced to in 1931. It is seen here outside, appropriately, Fulwell depot – its operational base throughout its 18-year service life. No 1 is now part of the London Transport Museum collection. *Marcus Eavis/Online Transport Archive*

Opposite below: **It is** 8 May 1962 and London's official last trolleybus – 'L3' class No 1521 – is seen at Fulwell depot suitably bedecked for the duty. No 1521 made the final ceremonial run over what had – at one stage – been the world's largest trolleybus system, finally returning to Fulwell depot in the early hours of 9 May. It was preserved after withdrawal, having been donated by George Cohen, the scrap merchant (who had initially purchased it), to the Historic Commercial Vehicle Club and now forms part of the collection held at the East Anglian Transport Museum. The origins of Fulwell depot itself lay with London United Tramways and opened originally in 1903. Closed to trams in October 1935, the depot accommodated trolleybuses throughout the thirty-one-year life of the system and, after 1962, was and remains in use as a bus garage. *Marcus Eavis/Online Transport Archive*

Fleet number	Registration	Chassis	Body	New	Withdrawn	Notes
1-35	HX2756/2755/3984/3983/3985/3986/3988/3987/4217//4220/4219/4218/4305/4306/4304/4303/4378-4375, HX125, MG100-103/125-128/187/183-186/350	AEC 663T	UCC H56R	1931	1948-51	'A1' class; ex-LUT; nicknamed 'Diddlers'; No 1 preserved
36-59	MG349/242-251/335-338/409-417	AEC 663T	UCC H56R	1931	1946-51	'A2' class; ex-LUT; nicknamed 'Diddlers'
60	MV1261	AEC 663T	UCC H56R	1931	1948	'A2' class (although also shown as 'X1')
61	AHX801	AEC 691T	LGOC H74	1933	1951	'X1' class (although also shown as 'A3')
62	AXU188	AEC 663T	MCCW H73R	1934	1952	'X2' class
63	AXU189	AEC 661T	EE H56R	1934	1952	'X3' class
64-93	CGF64-93	Leyland TTB2	BRCW H60R	1935-36	1955-59	'B1' class; rebuilt Fulwell late 1930s
94-131	CGF94-131	Leyland TTB2	Brush H60R	1935	1951-59 (99 wartime loss)	'B2' class; rebuilt Fulwell late 1930s; 95 and 107 rebuilt following war damage by Weymann in April 1942 being renumber 95A and 107A whilst 97 and 98 rebuilt following war damage by NCB in early 1946 and renumbered 97C and 98C; 94 and 106 rebuilt at Charlton in 1945 as a result of war damage
132-83	CGF132-183	AEC 664T	Weymann H70R	1935	1955	'C1' class; 138/42/48/75/83 sold to Georgetown Municipal Transport, Malaya, 1956

Fleet number	Registration	Chassis	Body	New	Withdrawn	Notes
184-283	CUL184-283	AEC 664T	MCCW H70R	1936	1955-59	'C2' class; 260 preserved
284-383	CUL284-383	AEC 664T	BRCW H70R	1936	1944-59 (364 destroyed by enemy action July 1944; 378 damaged January 1945 and rebuilt)	'C3' class
384	CUL384	Leyland	Leyland H70R	1936	1956	'D1' class
385-483	DGY385-483	Leyland	MCCW H70R	1936-37	1944-59 (386/87/94/98, 418/28/35/48 were wartime losses)	'D2' class; 406 destroyed Bexleyheath 1940 and rebuilt Weymann 1941 as D2A; 390-92/95, 405/07/09/51 destroyed at Bexleyheath and 412/70 at West Ham in 1944 and rebuillt by East Lancs as D2B during 1945 and 1946; 385/89/96/97, 402/15/19 destroyed at Bexleyheath and 430 at West Ham in 1944 and rebuilt by Northern Coachbuilders in 1946 as D2C
484-88	DGY484-488	Leyland	BRCW H60R	1936	1955	'B3' class
489-93	DGY489-493	Leyland	BRCW H60R	1936	1957-59	'B1' class
494-553	DLY494-553	Leyland	BRCW H70R	1937	1953-59	'D3' class
554-603	DLY554-603	AEC 664T	Brush H70R	1937	1955-60	'E1' class; 575/78 and 602 rebodied by NCB in 1946 following wartime damage and reclassified E1C

Fleet number	Registration	Chassis	Body	New	Withdrawn	Notes
604-28	DLY604-28	AEC 664T	Weymann H70R	1937	1956-60	'E2' class; 621 rebodied by Weymann 1942 and 623/26 by NCB following damage in West Ham Works July 1944 and reclassified as E2C.
629-53	DLY629-53	AEC 664T	PR H70R	1937	1955-59	'E3' class; 629/33/35/41/43 damaged July 1944 and rebodied by NCB and reclassified as 'E3C'
654-753	DLY654-753	Leyland	Leyland H70R	1937	1955-60	'F1' class
754	DLY754	AEC/ LPTB	LPTB H68R	1937	1955	'X4' class; first chassisless trolleybus acquired; also first (and only) trolleybus built by LPTB
755-904	ELB755-904	Leyland LPTB70	MCCW H70R	1937-38	1955-61 (787/91 and 812 were wartime losses)	'H1' class; 796 preserved
905-52	ELB905-52	AEC 664T	Weymann H70R	1937-38	1958-60	'J1' class
953	ELB953	AEC 664T	Weymann H70R	1938	1943	'M1' class; destroyed by fire
954	ELB954	AEC/ MCCW chassisless	MCCW H70R	1938	1961	'L2' class
955-1029	ELB955-999/EXX10/ EXV1-EXV29	AEC 664T	BRCW H70R	1938	1958-60	'J2' class; 1001 destroyed; 993, 1001A (rebodied by Weymann 1942) and 1007 rebodied by East Lancs 1947 due to war damage and reclassified 'J2B' with 'B' suffix to fleet number

Fleet number	Registration	Chassis	Body	New	Withdrawn	Notes
1030-054	EXV30-54	AEC 664T	BRCW H70R	1938	1960-61	'J3' class
1055-154/ 255-304	EXV55-154/255-304	Leyland LTB70	Leyland H70R	1938-39	1958-62	'K1' class; 1123, 1128 and 1285 rebodied by Weymann in 1941-42 due to war damage and reclassified 'K1A' with 'A' suffix to fleet number; 1123A further rebuilt 1946 by Beadle
1155-254/ 305-54	EXV155-254/305-354	Leyland LTB70	Leyland H70R	1938-39	1957-61	'K2' class; 1244 and 1247 rebodied by Weymann in 1941 due to war damage and reclassified 'K2A' with 'A' suffix to fleet number; 1246 also had minor rebuild following wartime damage; 1201, 1253 and 1348 preserved
1355-369	EXV355-369	AEC/ MCCW chassisless	MCCW H70R	1939	1959-61 (1365 wartime loss)	'L1' class
1370-378	EXV370-378	AEC/ MCCW chassisless	MCCW H70R	1939	1960-61	'L2' class
1379	EXV379	AEC/ MCCW chassisless	MCCW H69R	1939	1955	'X5' class
1380-529	FXF380/FXH381-529	AEC/ MCCW chassisless	MCCW H70R	1939-40	1959-62 (1492 and 1387 wartime losses)	'L3' class; 1385 rebuilt and rebodied by East Lancs in 1948 due to war damage and reclassified 'N1B' with 'B' suffix to fleet number; 1521 preserved
1530-554	FXH530-554	AEC/ MCCW 664T	Weymann	1939	1960-61	'M1' class; 1543 and 1545 rebuilt and rebodied by East Lancs in 1948 as a result of war damage and reclassified 'M1B' with 'B' suffix to fleet number

Fleet number	Registration	Chassis	Body	New	Withdrawn	Notes
1555-644	FXH555-644	AEC 664T	BRCW H70R	1939-40	1958-62	'N1' class; 1565 and 1587 rebodied by Weymann 1942 due to war damage and reclassified 'N1A' with 'A' suffix to fleet number
1645-669	FXH645-669	AEC 664T	PR H70R	1939-40	1956-62	'N2' class
1670	FXH670	AEC/EE chassisless	EE H68R	1940	1955	'X6' class
1671	DTD649	Leyland chassisless	Leyland H70R	1939	1955	'X7' class; built originally as Leyland demonstrator
1672-696	GCP672-696	Leyland	Leyland H70R	1940	1958-61	'K3' class
1697-721	GCP697-721	Leyland	MCCW H70R	1940-41	1960-61	'P1' class
1722-733	GGW722/GLB723-733	Leyland TTB	MCCW H72R	1941-42	1955-59	'SA1' class
1734-746	GLB734-746	Leyland TTB	MCCW H72R	1942	1959	'SA2' class
1747-764	GLB747-765	AEC 664T	MCCW H72R	1942-43	1959	'SA3' class
1765-891	HYM765-841/ LYH842-891	BUT 9641T	MCCW H70R	1948-53	1960-61	'Q1' class; all bar 1768/841 sold to Spain; 1768 and 1812 preserved in UK; 1836-839 survive in Spain
Wartime loans						
72-75/ 77-83/ 85-87/ 89, 117/ 23/45	AEL400-403/406-411/ALJ61-63/65/ ALJ991/997/ BEL830	Sunbeam MS2	Park Royal or EE H56D	1934-35	1941/42	Ex-Bournemouth Corporation; loaned December 1940; Nos 74, 75, 80, 81, 83, 85, 86, 89 and 117 returned to Bournemouth November 1941; remainder transferred to Newcastle September 1942

LUT Route number	From	To	Date Opened	Date Closed	Notes
1 (renumbered 601 August 1935)	Twickenham	Teddington	16 May 1931	N/A	
1 (renumbered 601 August 1935)	Teddington	Kingston Hill loop	15 June 1931	N/A	Service extended to Tolworth 15 July 1931
1A (renumbered 601A August 1935)	Surbiton	Tolworth (Red Lion)	15 July 1931	N/A	
1/2/3 (renumbered 601, 602 and 603 August 1935)	Tolworth (Red Lion)	Kingston Hill loop	15 July 1931	N/A	Originally routes 1 and 2; after opening of The Dittons service route 2 operated from The Dittons via Kingston Hill loop anticlockwise to Tolworth and route 3 operated from Tolworth clockwise via Kingston Hill loop to The Dittons until 20 September 1933
2/3 (renumbered 602 and 603 August 1935)	The Dittons	Kingston Hill loop	29 July 1931	N/A	Originally route 2; after opening of The Dittons service route 2 operated from The Dittons via Kingston Hill loop anticlockwise to Tolworth and route 3 operated from Tolworth clockwise via Kingston Hill loop to The Dittons until 20 September 1933
4 (renumbered 604 August 1935)	Wimbledon (Worple Road)	Hampton Court	2 September 1931	N/A	
4 (renumbered 604 August 1935)	Wimbledon (Worple Road)	Wimbledon (Town Hall)	15 December 1932	N/A	

LUT Route number	From	To	Date Opened	Date Closed	Notes
1/3 (renumbered 601 and 603 August 1935)	Tolworth (Red Lion)	Tolworth (Toby Jug)	20 September 1933	N/A	After extension opened Tolworth served by routes 1 and 3 and The Dittons by route 2
5 (renumbered 605 August 1935)	Malden	Teddington	1932	N/A	

LPTB Route number	From	To	Date Opened	Date Closed	Notes
513	Hampstead Heath	Holborn Circus	10 July 1938	31 January 1961	
517	Holborn	North Finchley	6 March 1938	31 January 1961	
521	Holborn	North Finchley	6 March 1938	7 November 1961	
543	Holborn	Wood Green	6 February 1939	18 July 1961	
555	Bloomsbury	Leyton	11 June 1939	14 April 1959	
557	Chingford Mount	Liverpool Street	11 June 1939	2 February 1960	
565	East Ham	Holborn	10 June 1940	16 October 1956	
567	Aldgate/ Smithfield	Barking	9 June 1940	10 November 1959	
569	Aldgate	Silvertown/ North Woolwich	23 July 1941 / 29 October 1941	10 November 1959	
581	Bloomsbury	Woodford	11 June 1939	14 April 1959	
601	Tolworth	Twickenham	October 1935	8 May 1962	
601A	Tolworth	Surbiton	October 1935	19 October 1943	
602	The Dittons	Kingston Hill loop	October 1935	8 May 1962	
603	Tolworth (Red Lion)	Kingston Hill loop	October 1935	8 May 1962	
604	Hampton Court	Wimbledon	October 1935	8 May 1962	
605	Malden	Teddington	October 1935	8 May 1962	Became Teddington to Wimbledon town hall 8 May 1940
607	Shepherds Bush	Uxbridge	15 November 1936	8 November 1960	
609	Barnet	Moorgate	6 March 1938	7 November 1961	
611	Highgate Village	Moorgate	10 December 1939	19 July 1960	

LPTB Route number	From	To	Date Opened	Date Closed	Notes
612	Battersea	Mitcham	12 September 1937	30 September 1950	Withdrawn in connection with the tram conversion programme
613	Holborn Circus	Parliament Hill Fields	10 July 1938	31 January 1961	513 worked from Hampstead Heath to Holborn Circus returning as a 613 to Parliament Hill Fields
615	Moorgate	Parliament Hill Fields	10 July 1938	31 January 1961	
617	Holborn	North Finchley	7 March 1938	31 January 1961	
621	Holborn	North Finchley	6 March 1938	7 November 1961	
623	Manor House	Woodford	18 October 1936	26 April 1960	
625	Wood Green	Woodford	8 May 1938	26 April 1960	The first route to include a section – Bruce grove to Ferry Road – not previously served by tram; became Woodford Winchmore Hill 12 October 1938
626	Acton	Clapham Junction	13 September 1937	19 July 1960	
627	Edmonton	Tottenham Court Road	6 November 1938	25 April 1961	Became Ponders End to TCR 6 November 1938; Archway to Smithfield 7 November 1938; Ponders End to TCR 24 October 1943; Waltham Cross to TCR 19 May 1954
628	Clapham Junction	Craven Park	12 September 1937	19 July 1960	Ran between Wembley (Triangle) and Clapham Junction between 4 August 1938 and 21 November 1939
629	Enfield	Tottenham Court Road	8 May 1938	25 April 1961	

LPTB Route number	From	To	Date Opened	Date Closed	Notes
630	Scrubs Lane	West Croydon	12 September 1937	19 July 1960	
639	Hampstead Heath	Moorgate	10 July 1938	31 January 1961	
641	Moorgate	Winchmore Hill	8 May 1938	7 November 1961	
643	Holborn	Wood Green	6 February 1939	18 July 1961	
645	Edgware	North Finchley	2 August 1936	2 January 1962	
645	Canons Park	Edgware	1 June 1938	2 January 1962	
645	Barnet	North Finchley	1 June 1938	2 January 1962	Replaced route 651
647	London Docks	Stamford Hill	5 February 1939	18 July 1961	
649	Ponders End	Stamford Hill	12 October 1938	18 July 1961	Became Waltham Cross to Liverpool Street 5 May 1948
649	Stamford Hill	Liverpool Street	5 February 1939	18 July 1961	Became Waltham Cross to Liverpool Street 5 May 1948; 649A was Sunday service from Wood Green to Liverpool Street
651	Barnet	Cricklewood	6 March 1938	31 May 1938	Replaced by extension of route 645
653	Aldgate	Tottenham Court Road	5 March 1939	31 January 1961	
654	Sutton	West Croydon	8 December 1935	3 March 1959	
654	Crystal Palace	West Croydon	9 February 1936	3 March 1959	
655	Hammersmith	Craven Park	13 December 1936	8 November 1960	Became Acton to Hammersmith 10 March 1937; Acton to Clapham Junction 12 September 1937; Acton Vale to Clapham Junction 10 July 1946
657	Hounslow	Shepherds Bush	27 October 1935	8 May 1962	
659	Holborn	Waltham Cross	16 October 1938	25 April 1961	

LPTB Route number	From	To	Date Opened	Date Closed	Notes
660	Hammersmith	Acton	5 April 1936	4 July 1936	
660	Hammersmith	North Finchley	2 August 1936	2 January 1962	
661	Aldgate	Leyton	5 November 1939	18 August 1959	
662	Paddington	Sudbury	23 August 1936	2 January 1962	
663	Aldgate	Ilford	5 November 1939	18 August 1959	Became Aldgate to Chadwell Heath 7 January 1959
664	Paddington	Edgware	23 August 1936	6 January 1959	
665	Barking	Bloomsbury	9 June 1940	10 November 1959	
666	Edgware	Hammersmith	5 July 1936	2 January 1962	
667	Hammersmith	Hampton Court	27 October 1935	8 May 1962	
669	Canning Town	Stratford	6 June 1936	2 February 1960	
669	Canning Town	North Woolwich	6 February 1938	2 February 1960	
677	Smithfield	West India Docks	10 September 1939	14 April 1959	
679	Ponders End	Smithfield	12 October 1938	25 April 1961	Became Waltham Cross to Smithfield 14 December 1938
683	Moorgate	Stamford Hill	5 February 1939	6 January 1959	
685	Leyton (Markhouse Road)	Walthamstow	17 January 1937	2 February 1960	Became Walthamstow to Canning Town 12 September 1937; Walthamstow to Silvertown 24 May 1939; Walthamstow to North Woolwich 8 May 1940; Walthamstow to Silvertown 13 April 1949; and, Walthamstow to North Woolwich 30 January 1952

LPTB Route number	From	To	Date Opened	Date Closed	Notes
687	Chingford Mount	Victoria & Albert Docks	6 June 1936	26 April 1960	Became Leyton depot to Victoria & Albert Docks 11 June 1939; Walthamstow to Victoria & Albert Docks 1 April 1942
689	Stratford circular		12 September 1937	2 February 1960	Operated via Plashet Grove and Green Street from 14 December 1937
690	Stratford circular		12 September 1937	2 February 1960	Operated via Green Street and Plashet Grove from 14 December 1937
691	Barking	Barkingside	6 February 1938	18 August 1959	
692	Chadwell Heath	The Horns	12 February 1938	3 December 1938	Saturdays only
693	Barking	Chadwell heath	6 February 1938	18 August 1959	
694	Erith	Woolwich Ferry via Welling	16 May 1937	28 May 1944	Sundays only
695	Chadwell Heath	Bow Church	29 October 1941	6 January 1959	
696	Dartford	Woolwich	10 November 1935	3 March 1959	Extended to Parsons Hill 14 July 1943
697	Chingford Mount	Victoria & Albert Docks	6 June 1936	26 April 1960	
698	Bexleyheath	Woolwich (Free Ferry)	10 November 1935	3 March 1959	Became Bexleyheath to Woolwich (Parsons Hill) 14 July 1943
699	Chingford Mount	Victoria & Albert Docks	6 June 1936	26 April 1960	

MAIDSTONE

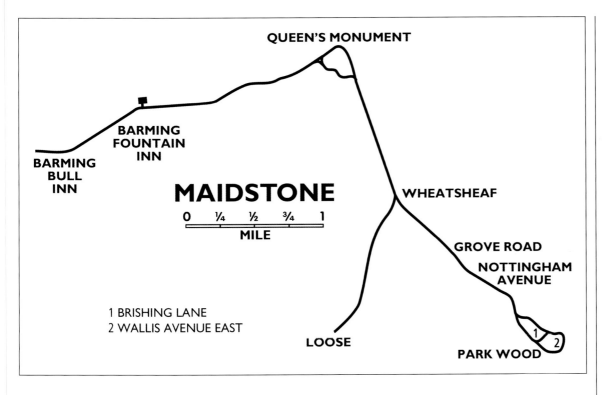

QUEEN'S MONUMENT

BARMING
FOUNTAIN
INN

BARMING
BULL
INN

MAIDSTONE

WHEATSHEAF

0   ¼   ½   ¾   1

MILE

GROVE ROAD

NOTTINGHAM
AVENUE

1 BRISHING LANE
2 WALLIS AVENUE EAST

LOOSE

PARK WOOD

1 2

I n 1904, Maidstone Corporation commenced operation of a 3ft 6in gauge tramway and, by the time the final extensions were opened in 1907, the network comprised three routes radiating out from the town centre to Barming, Loose and Tovil – a total of 5¼ route miles.

As elsewhere, by the early 1920s the operation of a relatively small system was proving problematic; track and equipment was becoming life-expired whilst new areas required some form of public transport. As a result, the corporation started to look at alternatives. On 18 July 1923, the Maidstone Corporation Act 1923 gained the Royal Assent; this, inter alia, permitted the corporation to operate both motorbuses and trolleybuses. Whilst the original Bill was progressing through parliament, representatives from Maidstone visited the then new Nechells route in Birmingham.

Although there were plans to introduce trolleybuses on the route from London Road to Penenden Heath, when the service was introduced on 7 April 1924 it was operated by motorbuses. Further bus services followed. However, indications that the track on the Barming route would need replacement by March 1928 at the latest – at some considerable (and uneconomic) cost – resulted in the decision to convert the route to trolleybus operation. The Maidstone Corporation (Trolley Vehicles) Order Confirmation was passed by parliament during the summer of 1927; this empowered the corporation

1946 and 1947. These were to be the last wholly new trolleybuses acquired by Maidstone and permitted the withdrawal of the three-axle vehicles; all of the latter had been taken out of service by the end of 1948.

After the war, Maidstone, in common with other towns and cities, saw the development of new housing in the suburbs; in particular development of a new council estate at Shephay – between Sutton Road and Mote Park – required the provision of public transport and the first proposals for an extension of the Sutton Road route were made in 1947. It was not, however, until March 1950 that it was agreed to proceed with the extension with the Ministry of Transport giving it approval in November 1951.

The nationalisation of the electricity supply industry from 1 April 1948 resulted in the corporation's power station at Fairmeadow passing to the newly created British Electricity Authority; thereafter, the corporation purchased its power requirements at the normal commercial rate. This left the transport department more vulnerable to external price increases, over which it had no control, rather than supporting another branch of the corporation.

The extension to serve the Park Wood estate opened in three stages: from the original terminus at Grove Road to Nottingham Avenue on 21 June 1954; from Nottingham Avenue to Brishing Lane on 4 May 1959; and, finally, from Brishing Lane to Wallis Avenue

During 1943 and 1944 Maidstone was allocated five Sunbeam Ws; Nos 54-58 were fitted with Park Royal-built Utility fifty-six-seat bodywork but were all to be rebodied by Roe during 1960. Here the first of the batch is seen in original condition outside Tonbridge Road (Barming) depot on 11 March 1951. The depot had its origins as a tram depot in 1904 and was extended some three years later. It was to be further enlarged in the late 1930s and accommodated the trolleybuses for the system's entire history. *John Meredith/Online Transport Archive*

East on 19 August 1963. The service through the Park Wood estate was effectively a giant loop with the overhead being removed from Brishing Lane when the final extension opened. The final extension took the Maidstone system to almost seven route miles – its maximum extent. Although further expansion was proposed, this did not take place. In order to cater for the additional services, a total of nine second-hand trolleybuses were acquired between 1955 and 1959 from Brighton, Hastings and Llanelly. The Llanelly duo, with their Utility bodywork, were not destined to remain in service for long, both being withdrawn by the end of 1960. Another alteration, in July 1963, saw the redesign of the loop at Loose. The town centre overhead was modified on 13 December 1964 with trolleybuses being introduced to the new Bishops Way and removed from Mill Street.

Although the system had only recently been extended and the five Utility-bodied trolleybuses rebodied, on 29 April 1964 it was agreed that the trolleybus system be converted to bus operation. The reasons cited – as elsewhere – included the problems of obtaining spares and the high cost of new vehicles. The conversion was scheduled over a four-year period. As new motorbuses were delivered, they gradually replaced the trolleybuses, running the existing timetables alongside the surviving trolleybuses. One of the consequences of the early withdrawals was the use of the small depot at Loose – which had last been used to accommodate vehicles in 1930 when the last trams were withdrawn – being pressed into use to store trolleybuses awaiting disposal.

The final replacement buses were delivered in early 1967 and, on 15 April, No 72 suitably decorated, acted as the official last trolleybus. The corporation had already decided that No 72 was to be preserved; indeed, it had undergone a late motor replacement shortly before closure to enable it to fulfil its last day duties. In addition to No 72, one of the rebodied Sunbeam Ws – No 56 – was also preserved whilst one each from the second-hand vehicles acquired from Brighton and Hastings were also saved.

Pictured post-rebuilding passing the now listed Ship Inn on Gabriel's Hill is one of the two Karrier Ws – No 55 – that was new in 1943. All five remained in service until the closure of the system on 15 April 1967 with No 54 acting as a duplicate to the official last trolleybus. One of the type – No 56 – was preserved following withdrawal. *Marcus Eavis/Online Transport Archive*

Above: **The last** new trolleybuses acquired by Maidstone were Nos 62-73; this was a batch of Sunbeam Ws supplied during 1946 and 1947 that were fitted with fifty-six-seat bodywork supplied by Northern Coachbuilders. When new only the offside cab windscreen opened; during the early 1950s the nearside windscreen was modified to permit opening as well. Additional ventilators were added to the front windows on the upper deck between 1959 and 1963. Of the twelve, seven – including No 69 seen here heading towards Barming (Bull Inn) – were withdrawn during 1965 with the other five remaining until 1967 (although one was dismantled prior to closure by the corporation for spares). No 72 was the official last trolleybus and was subsequently preserved. *Harry Luff/Online Transport Archive*

Right: **In 1952** Llanelly ceased trolleybus operation and put up for sale the twelve Karrier Ws with Utility bodywork that it had acquired during 1945 and 1946. Of these, ten went to Bradford, but Maidstone purchased two; these were Llanelly Nos 39 and 40 which, when they entered service in 1955 after a period of storage, became Maidstone Nos 84 and 85. The pair retained their Utility bodywork in Maidstone and were both withdrawn in October 1960 after the return of the last two of the rebodied Karrier Ws. *Harry Luff/Online Transport Archive*

Brighton Corporation acquired eight trolleybuses after the Second World War; these were all withdrawn in 1959, during the first phase of the system's conversion, and sold for further use. Two – ex-Brighton Nos 51 and 52 – were acquired by Maidstone, retaining their original Brighton numbers. Here No 52 is pictured on the Park Wood loop; the extension along Wallis Avenue East was the last opened on the system – on 19 August 1963 – and survived less than four years. No 52 is seen here after its front was damaged in an accident in August 1963. Operated on the last day, until it failed, No 52 was subsequently preserved. *Marcus Eavis/Online Transport Archive*

The third system from which Maidstone purchased vehicles second-hand was Hastings with five Sunbeam Ws with Weymann fifty-six-seat bodywork being acquired in 1959. These vehicles were part of a batch of fifteen delivered originally during 1947 that represented the last new trolleybuses acquired by Hastings Tramways. The five became Nos 85-89 in Kent and were to survive in service until 1966 (No 88) and 1967 (remainder); No 86 survives in preservation. Here No 87 – ex-Hastings No 35 – is seen at the Barming (Fountain Inn) short working on Tonbridge Road. *Harry Luff/Online Transport Archive*

Fleet number	Registration	Chassis	Body	New	Withdrawn	Notes
11-18	KO8891/8543/ 8544/8892-8896	RS&J D6	RS&J H63R	1928	1946-47	
23-29	KR351-357	EE	EE H56R	1930	1946-48	
54 and 55	GKN379-380	Sunbeam W	PR UH56R (rebodied by Roe [H62R] in 1960)	1943	1967	
56-58	GKP511-513	Sunbeam W	PR UH56R (rebodied by Roe [H62R] in 1960)	1944	1967	56 preserved
62-73	HKR1-12	Sunbeam W	NCB H56R	1946-47	1965-67	72 preserved
83 and 84	CBX522-523	Karrier W	Roe UH56R	1945	1960	Ex-Llanelly 39 and 40; acquired 1955
51 and 52	LCD51 and 52	BUT 9611T	Weymann H56R	1947 (bodied in 1951)	1966-67	Ex-Brighton 51 and 52; 52 preserved; acquired 1959
85-89	BDY807/809/ 810/817/818	Sunbeam W	Weymann H56R	1947	1965-67	Ex-Hastings 32, 34, 35, 42 and 43; acquired 1959; 86 preserved on withdrawal

Route number	From	To	Date Opened	Date Closed	Notes
N/A	Barming Fountain Inn	Centre	1 May 1928	15 April 1967	
N/A	Barming Bull Inn	Barming Fountain Inn	22 May 1947	15 April 1967	
N/A	Centre	Grove Road	12 February 1930	15 April 1967	
N/A	Centre	Loose	12 February 1930	15 April 1967	
N/A	Grove Road	Nottingham Avenue	21 June 1954	15 April 1967	
N/A	Nottingham Avenue	Park Wood (Brishing Lane)	4 May 1959	15 April 1967	
N/A	Park Wood (Brishing Lane)	Park Wood (Wallis Avenue East)	19 August 1963	15 April 1967	Loop along Brishing Lane removed with opening of extension

PORTSMOUTH

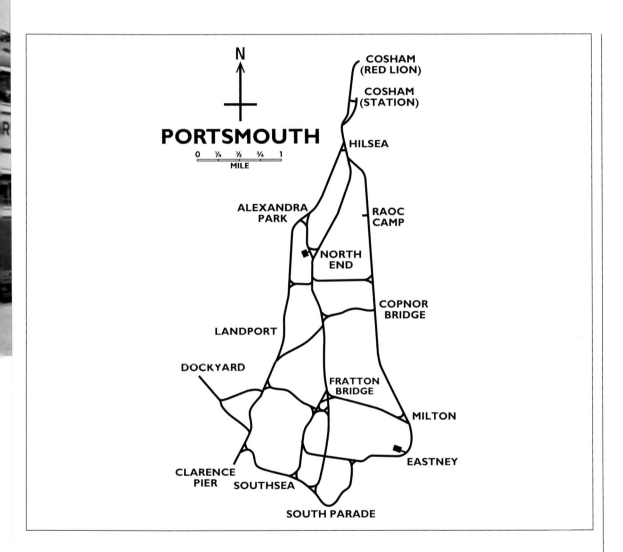

With its first section opening on 24 September 1901, the corporation-owned 4ft 7¾in gauge electric tramways eventually extended over almost 17¾ route miles. At Cosham a connection was made with the Portsdown & Horndean Tramway, owned by the Hampshire Light Railways (Electric) Co Ltd, which ran for some six miles northwards to Horndean and which eventually exercised running powers over Portsmouth track to the town hall on 1 August 1924 (extended to South Parade Pier on 19 April 1927).

The first proposals for the introduction of trolleybuses were made in the early 1920s but it was not until the Portsmouth Corporation Act 1930, which received the Royal Assent on 15 April 1930, that powers for the operation of trolleybuses were obtained. That year was

The Second World War resulted in a number of service reductions from July 1940 and four of the original trolleybuses from 1934 were loaned to Pontypridd Corporation between 1942 and 1946. The wartime service reductions were reversed on 1 July 1946 with new services being introduced. One facet of the Portsmouth system was the interlinked nature of many of the routes, which permitted an almost infinite variety of services to be operated. In the longer term another development of 1946 – the establishment of a 21-year co-ordination agreement with Southdown Motor Services – was eventually to have an impact on the trolleybus system.

The immediate post-war optimism saw a number of extensions proposed and further powers were obtained in the Portsmouth Corporation Act 1946, which received the Royal Assent on 26 July 1946, and the Portsmouth Corporation (Trolley Vehicles) Order Confirmation Act 1947. However, none of the proposed extensions were completed. Two of these proposals envisaged northern extensions from Cosham to the new Paulsgrove estate and to Farlington. In preparation for this, motorbuses took over operation of trolleybus services 1 and 2 on 18 May 1947, being extended to Farlington at the same time. This was the first trolleybus-to-motorbus conversion but did not involve any reduction in the trolleybus network as all the overhead affected was covered by other

The last of the initial group of fifteen trolleybuses was a second AEC 663T; unlike No 12, which was supplied with an English Electric sixty-seat body, No 215 (originally No 15) had a Metro-Cammell sixty-seat body. Pictured in 1949 inside North End depot during 1949, No 215 is seen towards the end of its life. No 212 was the first Portsmouth trolleybus to be withdrawn – in 1946 – with No 215 following in 1951. The majority of the trolleybuses delivered during 1934 were withdrawn during 1953 following the delivery of the new BUT 9611Ts. During their operational career, trolleybuses were housed in two depots – North End and Eastney – both of which had been previously used to accommodate trams. *Geoffrey Ashwell/Online Transport Archive*

Pictured at South Parade Pier on 10 August 1952 is No 219. This was one of a batch of nine AEC 661Ts fitted with English Electric fifty-seat bodywork that were delivered during 1935 as Nos 16-24 (they were renumbered 216-24 during 1938); these were the last trolleybuses acquired by Portsmouth to use bodywork from English Electric. All were withdrawn between 1950 and 1958. *John Meredith/Online Transport Archive*

services. The first reduction to the system occurred on 29 September 1951 when the section through the narrow streets from Guildhall to Floating Bridge was last operated by trolleybuses. Further powers were obtained in the Portsmouth Corporation (Trolley Vehicles) Order Confirmation Act 1952. However, Ben Hall, the general manager who had overseen the development of the system, retired in 1951 and his successor was much less pro-trolleybus.

The conversion of the Floating Bridge was more than compensated for two new extensions: Milton to Hilsea via Copnor on 25 May 1952 followed by the Chichester Road and Gladys Avenue sections on 27 September 1953. In addition, fifteen new trolleybuses were acquired during 1950 and 1951; these were the last new trolleybuses acquired as, three years later, proposals for the purchase of a further fifteen were rejected with motorbuses being substituted. Although there was no policy for conversion it was perhaps indicative of a change of emphasis.

The fate of the system was determined in 1956 when, following a recommendation by the general manager, it was agreed that the trolleybus network be converted to bus operation; this policy was reconfirmed the following year. There were a number of factors in the decision; these included the increased price of electricity, the complexity of the overhead (a consequence of the many interlinked routes) and improving co-ordination with Southdown (on 13 September 1958 the Cosham to South Parade Pier via Victoria

Road service was abandoned – again with no loss of overhead – to be replaced partially by an enhanced Southdown service). The necessary extensions to serve places like Paulsgrove were also deemed prohibitively expensive. Before the final go-ahead for conversion was given, however, consultants were employed but their report in 1959 confirmed the policy and, on 8 September 1959, the conversion programme was agreed.

The first routes to be converted – on 1 May 1960 – were those from Eastney to Alexandra Park via Gladys Avenue (ironically featuring the 1953 extensions) and Milton to Cosham via Eastney and Twyford Avenue. This was followed on 17 September 1960 by the service from Cosham to Green Lane via North End and Fratton. There was now a gap of over 12 months before, on 2 December 1961 services from Green Lane to Dockyard and to Clarence Pier via Fratton succumbed. There were no conversions during 1962 but the remaining routes were all converted – in two stages – during 1963 due to delays in the delivery of the replacement Leyland Atleanteans. The first of these, on 22 June, saw trolleybuses operate for the last time on the Dockyard to Dockyard circular service via Eastney and Milton. This left one service surviving – from Dockyard to Cosham via Southsea, Eastney and Copnor – which last operated on 27 July 1963. The last trolleybus in service was No 313; there was no official ceremony and all that marked No 313's role was a small notice in the front –upper-deck nearside window. Of the fleet, two examples – No 201 from the original batch in 1934 and No 313 from the post-war batch of BUT 9611Ts – survive in preservation.

Right: **In order** to facilitate the final conversion of the city's tram network, a further batch of AEC 661Ts was acquired during 1936 and 1937. Fitted with Craven-built fifty-two-seat bodywork, Nos 25-100 represented the single biggest order for trolleybuses placed by the corporation and were to become Nos 225-300 under the 1938 renumbering. Whilst the vast majority of the batch were rebuilt by the corporation using material supplied by Metal Sections between 1949, No 296 – seen here at Cosham in June 1953 – was not one of those so modified and, as a result, was one of the earliest to be withdrawn, succumbing during 1956. *Phil Tatt/Online Transport Archive*

Opposite above: **During 1950** and 1951, Portsmouth took delivery of a batch of fifteen BUT 9611Ts fitted with Burlingham fifty-two-seat bodywork; in the event these were to be the last new trolleybuses acquired by the corporation as plans to purchase a further fifteen new vehicles in 1954 came to nought as, by that date, the future of the network was under some doubt. Here one of the batch – No 310 – is pictured on The Hard having arrived with a service on route 6 from Cosham (Red Lion). The BUTs were all taken out of service between 1961 and 1963 with No 313 being preserved on withdrawal. *R.W.A. Jones/Online Transport Archive*

Opposite below: **In September** 1955, Portsmouth hosted the annual Municipal Passenger Transport Association conference and borrowed one of the then brand-new Sunbeam F4As fitted with Willowbrook seventy-seat bodywork that were then entering service with Walsall Corporation. On 1 October 1955 Walsall No 864 in seen on South Parade, Southsea, heading towards Cosham (Red Lion) with a service on route 5. *Gerald Druce/Online Transport Archive*

Two of the rebuilt pre-war AEC 661Ts are pictured on The Hard, the terminus that served the naval dockyard. On the right is No 230; as No 30 this was new in 1936 whilst No 298 (originally No 98) on the left was one of the last ten delivered the following year. Both of the trolleybuses were withdrawn in 1961; the last of the type survived into 1963. *Marcus Eavis/ Online Transport Archive*

During 1950 and 1951 Portsmouth took delivery of a batch of fifteen Burlingham-bodied BUT 9611Ts; although there were proposals in 1954 for a the purchase of a further fifteen new trolleybuses, uncertainties as to the system's future led to an order for additional new motorbuses instead with the result that Nos 301-15 were destined to be Portsmouth's last new trolleybuses. Typical of the batch is No 309, which is pictured here at the Dockyard terminus. The first casualty was No 303, which was withdrawn following a serious accident in Milton Road during April 1961, but the remainder survived until the final conversion of the system in July 1963. The final trolleybus in service was No 313; the only commemoration was a small notice in the front upper-deck nearside window. There was to be no official farewell other than this. Following the closure, No 313 was secured for preservation. *Harry Luff/Online Transport Archive*

Fleet number	Registration	Chassis	Body	New	Withdrawn	Notes
1-4 (renumbered 201-04 1938)	RV4649-4652	AEC 661T	EE H50R	1934	1955-58	201 preserved
5-7 renumbered 205-07 1938)	RV4653-4655	Leyland TBD2	EE H50R	1934	1953	
8 (renumbered 208 1938)	RV4656	Sunbeam MF2	EE H50R	1934	1953	
9 (renumbered 209 1938)	RV4657	Karrier E4	EE H50R	1934	1953	
10 (renumbered 210 1938)	RV4660	Sunbeam MF2	MCCW H50R	1934	1953	
11 (renumbered 211 1938)	RV4661	Karrier E4	MCCW H50R	1934	1953	
12 (renumbered 212 1938)	RV4658	AEC 663T	EE H50R	1934	1946	Loaned to Pontypridd during the Second World War; stored on return until disposal in 1954
13 (renumbered 213 1938)	RV4659	Sunbeam MS3	EE H50R	1934	1953	Loaned to Pontypridd during the Second World War
14 (renumbered 214 1938)	RV4662	Sunbeam MS3	MCCW H50R	1934	1953	Loaned to Pontypridd during the Second World War
15 (renumbered 215 1938)	RV4663	AEC 663T	MCCW H50R	1934	1951	Loaned to Pontypridd during the Second World War
16-24 (renumbered 216-24 1938)	RV6374-6382	AEC 661T	EE H50R	1935	1950-58	
25-100 (renumbered 225-300 1938)	RV8307-8336/9106-9145/9149-9154	AEC 661T	Cravens H52R (all bar 240, 257, 258, 262-64, 266, 272, 276, 279, 280, 284, 275, 287-89 and 296 rebuilt by the corporation 1948-56 using parts supplied by Metal Sections)	1936-37	1951-61	
301-15	ERV926-940	BUT 9611T	Burlingham H52R	1950-51	1961-63	313 preserved

Route number	From	To	Date Opened	Date Closed	Notes
3/4	Cosham	South Parade Pier (via Fawcett Road, Fratton Road and London Road)	4 August 1934	17 July 1940	5 July 1940 ceased to serve Sea Front due to wartime restrictions; replaced by 3/4A and 3A/4 17 July 1940 – see below
3/4	South Parade Pier	Cosham via Albert Road, Guildhall, Twyford Avenue, Northern Parade and Hilsea)	3 November 1935	17 July 1940	5 July 1940 ceased to serve Sea Front due to wartime restrictions; replaced by 3/4A and 3A/4 17 July 1940 – see below
1/2	Cosham	Clarence Pier (via Guildhall)	1 October 1936	17 May 1947	5 July 1940 ceased to serve Sea Front due to wartime restrictions; diverted to operate via Osborne Road and Victoria Road; replaced by new services 7/8, 9/10 and 13/14 1 July 1946 – see below
11/12	Copnor Bridge	Dockyard (via Lake Road)	1 November 1936	2 December 1961	Extended to Green Lane (Madeira Road) (via Copnor Road) 6 January 1952
15/16	Copnor Bridge	Floating Bridge (via Lake Road)	1 November 1936	29 September 1951	Cut back to run Copnor Bridge to Guildhall 17 July 1940 due to wartime restrictions
5/6	Dockyard	Guildhall (via South Parade Pier and Eastney)	10 November 1936	17 July 1940	5 July 1940 ceased to serve Sea Front due to wartime restrictions
17/18	Dockyard	Dockyard (via Eastney and Milton)	10 November 1936	22 June 1963	
3A/4 (renumbered 19/20 26 September 1948)	Cosham	Guildhall (via Guildhall, Albert Road and Milton)	17 July 1940	1 May 1960	

Route number	From	To	Date Opened	Date Closed	Notes
3/4A renumbered 3/4 26 September 1948)	Cosham	Dockyard (via Fratton Road and The Strand)	17 July 1940	17 September 1960	Extended to South Parade Pier 13 May 1945 and to Alexandra Park (via Twyford Avenue) 1 July 1946
1A/2A (renumbered 1/2 18 May 1947)	Cosham	Eastney (via Guildhall and Palmerston Road)	17 July 1940	18 June 1950	
5/6	Dockyard	Milton (via Southsea)	13 May 1945	27 July 1963	Extended to Cosham (Red Lion) (via Milton Road and Copnor Road) 25 May 1952
7/8	Copnor Bridge	Clarence Pier (via Fawcett Street and The Strand)	1 July 1946	2 December 1961	Extended to Green Lane (Madeira Road) (via Copnor Road) 6 January 1952
9/10	Cosham	Cosham (via Victoria Road and Guildhall)	1 July 1946	26 September 1953	Initially suspended; never reinstated
13/14	Cosham	South Parade Pier (via Victoria Road)	1 July 1946	13 September 1958	
15/16	Alexandra Park	Eastney (via Chichester Road)	27 September 1953	1 May 1960	

On 14 July 1953 No 264 is seen awaiting departure from the terminus at Cosham railway station. This was Cravens-bodied AEC 661Ts of 1936/37 that was not rebuilt by the corporation between 1948 and 1956. *Gerald Druce/Online Transport Archive*

READING

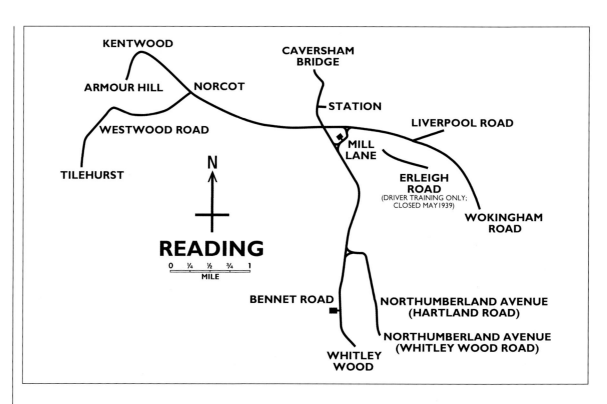

From 1903 Reading Corporation operated a relatively small – almost 7½ route mile at its peak – 4ft 0in gauge electric tramway. Early in the following decade, with the expansion of the borough's boundaries, there were the first initial proposals for trolleybus services to serve the newly incorporated areas and powers for this were included in the Reading Corporation Act 1914 which received the Royal Assent on 31 July 1914. The date was not propitious as the outbreak of the First World War the following month meant little progress other than a quote for the supply of vehicles being obtained. In December 1919 the corporation introduced its first motorbus route, and it was to be a decade before trolleybuses were seriously considered again.

By the late 1920s, the tramway needed investment to replace track and rolling stock. In 1929 the general manager, James McLennan Calder, produced a report on the future of the Oxford Road tramway. He concluded that trolleybuses were an option, but nothing progressed again initially. In the meantime, the first tramway conversions – to motorbus – took place on the Bath Road route in 1930 and the Erleigh Road on 7 August 1932. By this date, however, the use of trolleybuses was again being seriously considered and visits were undertaken to a number of systems.

Following this research, a report was presented on 3 May 1934; this recommended that powers be obtained under the 1914 Act to permit the operation of trolleybuses on a

In 1936, Reading Corporation took delivery of six trolleybuses from five different manufacturers; two were Sunbeam MF2As, including one that had previously been used as a demonstrator, whilst the others came from AEC, Guy, Leyland and Ransomes, Sims & Jefferies. Originally Nos 1-6, the vehicles were renumbered 101-06 during 1938. No 102 – seen here after withdrawal in storage at the new Bennet Road depot on 23 December 1950 – was an AEC 661T and, like the other five, had bodywork supplied by Park Royal. Of the six, four were withdrawn during 1949 following the delivery of Nos 138-57 whilst the other two following in 1950 with the arrival of Nos 170-81. No 102 was withdrawn at the end of October 1950 and sold for scrap in January 1951. *John Meredith/Online Transport Archive*

number of routes. This was adopted as corporation policy and, on 2 August 1935, Royal Assent was given to the Reading Corporation Act 1935. This was followed by the granting of a Provisional Order the following year. With powers in place, work commenced on the construction of the initial route from Caversham Bridge to Whitley Bridge. The first overhead to be erected – on 5 December 1935 – covered a detached section on Erleigh Road; this was used for the training of drivers and, never being connected to the main network, was never used to provide a public service.

With the first vehicles delivered – six of varied chassis construction but all fitted with Park Royal bodywork – and the official Ministry of Transport inspection on 14 July 1936, trams were withdrawn from the Caversham to Whitley route on 15 July 1936, with the trolleybuses being officially inaugurated three days later. This left two main tramway services still operational: west along Oxford Road and east along Wokingham Road with a branch along London Road. In order to convert these services, the corporation ordered twenty-five trolleybuses from AEC; these were delivered between December 1938 and April 1939. Due to low bridges on Caversham Road and Oxford Road, the corporation had to obtain special dispensation from the Ministry of Transport for the use of these highbridge vehicles as the overhead clearance was lower than normally permitted.

For the opening of the sections to Liverpool Road, Wokingham Road and Tilehurst in May 1939, Reading acquired twenty-five AEC 661Ts with Park Royal fifty-six-seat bodywork. Nos 107-31 were delivered between December 1938 and March 1939 with the first being used for driver training from January. In the early 1950s, six – Nos 107-12 – were withdrawn with a view to disposal but were stored until re-entering service between 1952 and January 1957 mainly in place of the ex-Huddersfield Karriers. Final withdrawal of the type commenced in June 1958 when, as a result in a decline in traffic, a number were taken out of traffic. A total of eleven had succumbed by the end of September 1958; the remaining fourteen were withdrawn following the purchase of Nos 182-93 in 1961. No 113 was preserved following withdrawal. Here No 125, one of those withdrawn in 1958, is seen approaching the terminus at Tilehurst on 1 July 1951. *John Meredith/Online Transport Archive*

To accommodate the new trolleybuses an extension to the existing depot at Mill Lane was completed; this was completed on 31 October 1938.

The new routes were officially inspected on 16 May 1939 and, on 20 May 1939, Reading's last tram operated. Trolleybuses took over operation took over the following day with services on the Oxford Road route being extended through to Tilehurst.

During the Second World War, the municipal power station, which had been situated adjacent to the depot at Mill Lane, was closed and the boiler house was converted to a workshop for trolleybus maintenance. The fleet was increased in 1943 by the arrival of

The first new trolleybuses delivered to Reading post-war were twenty BUT 9611Ts – Nos 138-57 – that were fitted with Park Royal fifty-six-seat bodies. The batch was delivered between March and June 1949 in order to facilitate the extensions planned for later that year. These were the first trolleybuses operated by Reading that were built to the new maximum permitted width – 8ft 0in – and also included a number of innovations – such as driver-operated platform doors and deeper windscreens that had been designed by the general manager, W.J. Evans. All were withdrawn between January 1967 and March 1968 as the system contracted with the exception of No 144, which was retained and repainted to act as the official last trolleybus on 3 November 1968; it was subsequently preserved. Typical of the batch is No 145, one of those withdrawn in December 1966 as result of the conversion of the Whitley Wood route, which is pictured here at Kentwood, adjacent to Tilehurst station. *Harry Luff/Online Transport Archive*

six Sunbeam W4s fitted with Park Royal Utility bodywork. The new arrivals helped to cater for the growth of traffic during the war and also strengthened the fleet for the only extension to open during the war – that from Norcot to Kentwood (adjacent to Tilehurst station) on 31 July 1944 – where the trolleybuses replaced the inadequate motorbus service. In 1945, McLennan retired; he was replaced by William Morrison Little who had been general manager at St Helens. In 1946, Little departed as general manager to take over as general manager at Edinburgh (where he oversaw the conversion of the city's tramway network to motorbus operation); he was replaced by William John Evans from

In the late 1940s, in order to cater for a boom in traffic post-war, Reading Corporation sought to supplement its fleet; taking advantage of the fact that Huddersfield was disposing of its first production batch of trolleybuses – Nos 7-18 (later 407-18) – which were Karrier E6s dating originally from 1934. These vehicles, which had largely been relegated to peak hour duties from 1941 as non-standard, were purchased for £400 each. Of the twelve purchased, the original plan was to refurbish ten for service, but this was subsequently reduced to six – Nos 158-63 – with two being scrapped at Mill Lane with the other four being dismantled at Bennet Road in May 1952. The quartet eventually scrapped in 1952 are seen here awaiting their fate on 23 December 1950. *John Meredith/Online Transport Archive*

Cardiff. Whilst in his previous position as chief engineer and joint manager, he had overseen the introduction of trolleybuses to that city in 1942.

After the war, it was agreed to extend the system further, with powers for a number of sections being enshrined within the Reading Corporation (Trolley Vehicles) Order Confirmation Act 1946, which received the Royal Assent on 1 August 1946. The late 1940s witnessed the opening of three extensions. On 5 June 1949, the Whitley Street service was extended to Northumberland Avenue. This was followed on 7 August 1949 by a branch off the Caversham Bridge route to serve the main railway stations and one off the Northumberland Avenue route to Whitley Wood. In order to operate these new services, twenty new BUT 9611Ts were acquired along with twelve second-hand Karrier E6s from Huddersfield (although only half of the latter entered service). In 1950 a further twelve new vehicles – this time Sunbeam S7s fitted with Park Royal bodywork – were delivered.

One of the six ex-Huddersfield Karrier E6s fitted Brush fifty-six-seat bodywork – No 160 – makes use of the reverser at the Whitley Wood terminus on 21 February 1953. The six were withdrawn finally between October 1955 and December 1956, with No 160 succumbing in August 1956. They were replaced in service by the stored AEC 661Ts – Nos 107-11 – that had been taken out of service earlier in the decade. No 112 was restored to service in 1952 following the withdrawal on No 126 following the latter's overturning. The Whitley Wood route was one of the extensions opened on 7 August 1949; it was to remain trolleybus operated until 8 January 1967. *John Meredith/Online Transport Archive*

From 14 January 1952 the depot at Bennet Road was brought into use officially, completed two years earlier, it had been used for storage initially. This depot was to prove something of a white elephant, never being fully utilised and was closed on 24 October 1958.

The mid-1950s saw a number of possible extensions proposed and, in October 1956, it was agreed to seek powers for this work. At the same time a report was prepared on the future of the system; the decision was to retain the system and acquire new vehicles; at that stage, despite the tide elsewhere turning against the trolleybus, the report saw a future for the system extending into the early 1980s. The new extensions were covered in the Reading Corporation (Trolley Vehicles) Provisional Order Act 1957, which received the Royal Assent on 31 July 1957. The new extension from Kentwood to Armour Hill opened on 4 August 1958.

In furtherance of the policy agreed in 1957, a further batch of new trolleybuses was ordered; these were twelve Sunbeam F4As fitted with Burlingham bodywork. However, due to delays, these did not enter service until 1961 and were to be the last new trolleybuses acquired by Reading. The same year saw the first appearance on the vehicles of the route letters; these had been used internally previously (the route letters were to be replaced by route numbers in 1964). Two years later – on 14 January 1963 – the system saw its final expansion with the extension of the Northumberland Avenue route from its original terminus

Acquired in 1950, Nos 170-181 represented a batch of Sunbeams S7s fitted with Park Royal sixty-eight-seat bodywork. The trolleybuses were deigned to replace both the original six vehicles acquired in 1936 as well as the Utility-bodied Karrier Ws of 1943 (Nos 132-37). Before entering service, No 174 was exhibited at the 1950 Commercial Motor Transport Exhibition. As a result of their weight the batch was not permitted normally to operate the Whitley routes, although two were not allowed on the Bridge Street bridge at the same time due to weight restrictions. The restriction was lifted later in the 1950s when the bridge was strengthened. Here No 175 is seen using the loop at the Wokingham Road (Three Tuns) terminus on 30 March 1966. The first withdrawal of the batch occurred in December 1967 but eight survived until November 1968. Two – Nos 174 and 181 – were preserved whilst a third – No 170 – was used as an additional classroom by Sonning Church of England Primary School from 1969 until 1976; it was then scrapped. *Alan Murray-Rust/Online Transport Archive*

located about 400 yards south of the roundabout at Hartland Road to a new terminus at Whitley Wood Road. The same year saw work undertaken on the major construction of Wokingham Road with the work designed to accommodate the trolleybus service.

In late 1964 and early 1965, traffic congestion led to plans for a one-way system in the town centre; initially these included the possibility of erecting overhead in Greyfriars Road. The work was undertaken and the new one-way loop was opened on 11 July 1965. The previous day, however, had seen the first contraction with the conversion – approved in March 1965 on financial grounds – of the route to Caversham Bridge. Although there was still no policy for complete conversion, this was to change following the local council elections of 1966; the new council decided on 26 July 1966 to support a policy of conversion.

The next route to be converted – on 8 January 1967 – was the route to Whitley Wood. The spring of 1967 saw the retirement of Evans as general manager; his replacement was Royston C. Jenkins who had previously been deputy general manager at Middlesbrough. The Northumberland Avenue route was followed on 31 December 1967 by the route from Whitley Wood Road to the Stations; this included the recently completed diversion via Greyfriars Road. The penultimate state in the programme – on 3 March 1968 – saw

The final trolleybuses purchased by Reading were twelve Sunbeam F4As – Nos 182-93 – that entered service between June and September 1961. Fitted with sixty-eight-seat forward-entrance bodywork supplied by Burlingham, the batch was designed to replace the surviving AEC 661Ts of 1939. On 3 September 1968, towards the end of the system's life, No 185 is recorded heading along Wokingham Road with a service towards Tilehurst; No 185 was one of five of the batch to be sold to Tees-side Municipal Transport for further use following the final abandonment of the Reading system. Of the remainder, six were scrapped whilst No 193 was secured for preservation. Subsequently, one of those sold to Tees-side – No 186 (Tees-side No T291; now restored to its original Teesside livery and number [11] at Beamish) – was also preserved, although it has retained its Tees-side livery in preservation. *Geoffrey Tribe/Online Transport Archive*

the conversion of the services to Liverpool Road and Armour Hill (although the latter section saw use for the final time on 10 March 1968 when traversed by a special). This left one remaining service – from the Three Tuns on Wokingham Road to Tilehurst; this was expected to be converted during the summer of 1968 but, in the event, the route survived until 3 November 1968 with No 144 acting as the official last trolleybus.

Of the Reading fleet, five of the 1961 batch of Sunbeams were sold to the Teesside Railless Traction Board (with one subsequently being secured for preservation, whilst five other Reading vehicles – Nos 113, 144, 174, 181 and 193 – also survive.

Fleet number	Registration	Chassis	Body	New	Withdrawn	Notes
1 (Renumbered 101 in 1938)	RD8085	Sunbeam MF2A	PR L50R	1933	1949	Built as a demonstrator originally and displayed at the 1933 Commercial Motor Transport Exhibition; it was acquired by Reading in March 1936
2 (Renumbered 102 in 1938)	RD8086	AEC 661T	PR L52R	1936	1950	
3 (Renumbered 103 in 1938)	RD8087	Guy BT	PR L52R	1936	1949	
4 (Renumbered 104 in 1938)	RD8088	Leyland TB4	PR L52R	1936	1949	
5 (Renumbered 105 in 1938)	RD8089	RS&J	PR L52R	1936	1949	
6 (Renumbered 106 in 1938)	RD8090	Sunbeam MF2A	PR L52R	1936	1950	
107-31	ARD670-694	AEC 661T	PR H56R	1939	1952-61	113 preserved
132-37	BRD797-801/14	Sunbeam W	PR UH56R	1943	1950	
138-57	DRD124-143	BUT 9611T	PR H56RD	1949	1966-68	144 preserved
158-69	VH6757/6753/ 6751/6759/6755/ 6752/6761/6760/ 6754/6750/6758/ 6756	Karrier E6	Brush H64R	1934	1955-56	Ex-Huddersfield 14, 10, 8, 16, 12, 9, 18, 17, 11, 7, 15 an 13 respectively; acquired 1948; only 158-63 entered service with remainder scrapped during 1951 and 1952
170-81	ERD141-152	Sunbeam S7	PR H68RD	1950	1967-68	174 and 181 preserved
182-93	VRD182-193	Sunbeam F4A	Burlingham H68F	1961	1968	183-86/92 sold to TRTB; 193 preserved; 186 preserved as TRTB 11

Route number	From	To	Date Opened	Date Closed	Notes
E (15 from 9 August 1964)	Centre	Caversham Bridge	18 July 1936	10 July 1965	Closed between junction for Stations branch and terminus
D 16 from 9 August 1964)	Centre	Whitley Street	18 July 1936	31 December 1967	
C (18 from 9 August 1964)	Cemetery Junction	Liverpool Road	21 May 1939	3 March 1968	
A (17 from 9 August 1964)	Centre	Wokingham Road (Three Tuns)	21 May 1939	3 November 1968	
A (17 from 9 August 1964)	Centre	Tilehurst	21 May 1939	3 November 1968	
C (18 from 9 August 1964)	Norcot	Kentwood	31 July 1944	3 March 1968	
E (15 from 9 August 1964)	Whitley Street	Northumberland Avenue (Hartland Road)	5 June 1949	31 December 1967	
E (15 from 9 August 1964)	Caversham Road	Stations	7 August 1949	31 December 1967	
D (16 from 9 August 1964)	Whitley Street	Whitley Wood	7 August 1949	8 January 1967	
C (18 from 9 August 1964)	Kentwood	Armour Hill	4 August 1958	3 March 1968	
E (15 from 9 August 1964)	Northumberland Avenue (Hartland Road)	Northumberland Avenue (Whitley Wood Road)	14 January 1963	31 December 1967	
15	Stations	West Street (via Greyfriars Road)	11 July 1965	31 December 1967	Overhead erected in connection with one-way system
N/A	Erleigh Road (Craven Road)	Erleigh Road (Eastern Avenue)	Spring 1936	May 1939	Used for driver training only; not dismantled until February 1955)

For its experimental service from Victoria Circus to Prittlewell (operated alongside the existing trams), Southend hired two Short Bros-bodied Railless vehicles; Nos 1 – illustrated here when new – and 2 were delivered during 1925 and 1926. Purchased by the corporation, the pair were renumbered 101 and 102 in 1927. The pair survived in service until withdrawal in 1933. *R. Sims/J. Joyce Collection/Online Transport Archive*

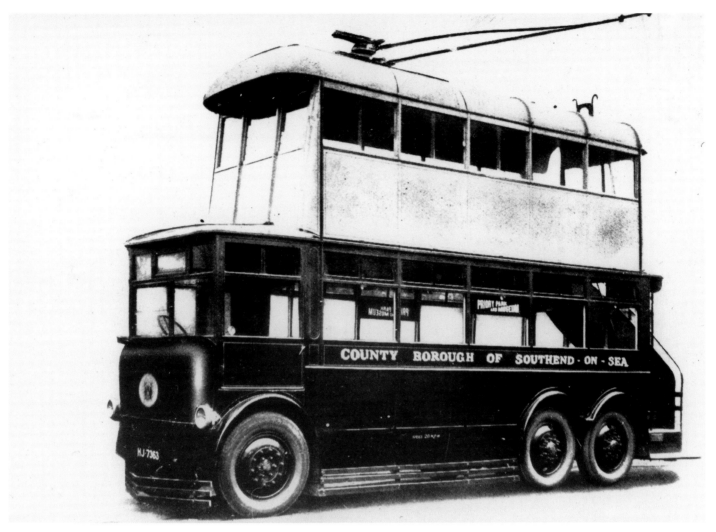

The first three trolleybuses acquired by Southend were all single-deck; the first double-decker to be acquired was No 104, which was delivered in 1928. This had a chassis supplied by Garrett with an open-staircase body supplied by the same manufacturer. Pictured here when new, No 104 was withdrawn in 1939. *Barry Cross Collection/Online Transport Archive*

Additional powers were obtained courtesy of the Southend-on-Sea Corporation (Trolley Vehicles) Provisional Order Act 1927, which received the Royal Assent on 27 May 1927, and the Southend-on-Sea Corporation (Trolley Vehicles) Provisional Order Act 1929, which received the Royal Assent on 21 March 1929. A short extension to Bankside – along White Gate Road – opened on 12 December 1928, due to the LMS not permitting the construction of a terminal loop in the station forecourt, but a low railway bridge to the east of Southend Central station prevented the route opening to the Kursaal for the sea front until the road under the bridge had been lowered. This was completed and the Kursaal extension opened on 2 August 1929, the day after it had been officially inspected.

Further legislation for the extension of the system was enshrined in the Southend-on-Sea Corporation Act 1930, which received the Royal Assent on 1 August 1930, which covered nine sections of route.

One of the routes authorised in the 1930 Act was from the existing Prior Park route along Fairfax Drive to Eastwood Boulevard; this opened on 21 January 1932. This section had not previously been operated by tram. Another new route followed on 31 July 1932 with the opening of the route to Hamstel Road via North Avenue.

The story of public transport in Southend is complicated by the fact that the development of local motorbus services, particularly after the passing of the Road Traffic Act of 1930 (which brought in licensing of bus services), was subject to an agreement with local bus operators in 1932 whereby the corporation could develop motorbus services to the east whilst companies like Westcliff-on-Sea Motor Services could operate in the west. As both tram and trolleybus services were covered by statute, they were protected from this agreement.

On 21 June 1934, a short extension from the Kursaal route westwards along Marine Parade to the Pier Head was opened. The same year also saw the decision made to extend the Kursaal route to Thorpe Bay; powers to achieve this were granted in the Southend-on-Sea Corporation (Trolley Vehicles) Provisional Order Act 1934, which received the Royal Assent on 17 May 1934 although it would be some five years before the extension finally opened. The next extension – on 24 July 1935 – saw the Eastwood Boulevard service extended to Wellington Avenue.

At this stage there was no still definite plan for the conversion of the remaining tram routes. Although the last new trams – six supplied by English Electric – had been delivered in 1923, the corporation had purchased six second-hand trams – three from Middlesbrough and three from Accrington (all of which had had to be regauged before re-entering service) – in 1934 and it was not until 1938 that the final decision to convert the remaining tram routes was agreed. One factor in the decision was the poor state of the track and the costs involved in replacing it. A further piece of legislation – the

In 1930, Southend took delivery of two English Electric chassis – Nos 110 and 111 – that were equipped with the same manufacturer's fifty-six-seat bodywork. Here No 110 is pictured when new. In 1937, the seating on the two vehicles was modified, when the front doorway was eliminated and, two years later, the pair was sold to Nottingham Corporation where they became Nos 302 and 303. Both were withdrawn by Nottingham in 1945. *Roy Marshall/The Bus Archive*

During 1932 and 1933 Southend Corporation purchased a total of nine AEC 661Ts – Nos 112-15/17-21 – fitted with English Electric forty-eight-seat bodywork. All were – like No 115 illustrated here – originally equipped with fake radiators but all – with the exception of Nos 112 and 115 – were subsequently modified post-war to lose this feature. All were withdrawn from service during 1950 (Nos 112/15-17) and 1954 (remainder). *John Meredith Collection/Online Transport Archive*

Southend-on-Sea Corporation (Trolley Vehicles) Provisional Order Act 1939, which received the Royal Assent on 8 May 1939 – permitted the conversion of the surviving routes to trolleybus operation.

The first conversion, however, predated that Act when, on 6 July 1938 motorbuses replaced trams on the route to Thorpe Bay from Southchurch and Bournes Green. This left the tram network as Leigh-on-Sea to Southchurch or to Thorpe Bay via the Kursaal. However, in December 1938 work commenced on the conversion of the Kursaal to Thorpe Bay service and on, 3 June 1939, trams ceased to operate east of the Kursaal; trolleybuses took over the section on the following day.

As elsewhere, the outbreak of war in September 1939 resulted in changed priorities and gave the surviving tram routes a reprieve. However, as the war progressed, the condition of the tram track continued to deteriorate. A number of the trolleybuses were loaned to Bradford early in the war as traffic in Southend declined (the section to Thorpe Bay was regarded as a summer only service and was suspended for the duration of hostilities); as these were returned, the possibility of using them to replace the remaining trams was agreed during the summer of 1941. In order to release overhead for the conversion of the remainder of the tram network, the tram service from Southchurch Road to the Southchurch terminus was withdrawn on 7 January 1942. This reduced the tram service to a single route – Leigh to the Kursaal – and work proceeded on the conversion of the section from Wellington Avenue to the Kursaal; although powers existed for the operation of trolleybuses from Chalkwell Hall Schools to Leigh-on-Sea, this section was never operated by trolleybus.

The final trams operated on 8 April 1942 and, on the same day, trolleybuses commenced operation on the route. The completion of the section from the town centre to Wellington Avenue permitted the introduction of the western circular service. The next extension saw trolleybuses introduced over the erstwhile tram route along Southchurch Road to Southchurch (White Horse); in addition, a new connection was opened between Southchurch and the junction between North Avenue and Hamstel Road; this had the effect of creating a second eastern circular service and led to the abandonment of the original Hamstel Road terminus. A new short working – provided with a reverser – was opened via short spur in Lonsdale Road, to the west of the junction in 1945.

After the war, the corporation gained further powers in the Southend-on-Sea Corporation Act 1947, which received the Royal Assent on 31 July 1947; this Act stated:

Two of the 1933 batch of AEC 661Ts – Nos 118 on the left and 117 on the right – are pictured at the corporation's London Road depot towards the end of their life. Of the five delivered during 1933, the remaining three – Nos 119-21 – were rebuilt during 1945 without their dummy radiators and were to survive until 1954; Nos 117 and 118, which remained unmodified through their operational life, were both withdrawn in 1950. *Geoffrey Ashwell/Online Transport Archive*

And whereas the Corporation are the owners of and are working a system of trolley vehicles within the borough and by the Southend-on-Sea Corporation (Trolley Vehicles) Order 1942 made by the Minister of War Transport in virtue of his powers under the Defence (General) Regulations 1939 the Corporation were empowered to provide equip maintain and use trolley vehicles along the route in the borough therein mentioned and it is expedient that the powers of the Corporation should be confirmed and that they should be empowered to provide equip maintain and use trolley vehicles along a new trolley vehicle route within the borough: And whereas it is expedient to confer further powers on the Corporation in regard to their trolley vehicles public service vehicles and electricity undertakings.

However, events elsewhere meant that no further routes were developed; discussions were taking place with Westcliff-on-Sea Motor Services and with Eastern National over a joint traffic agreement in which the trolleybuses would have no place. The agreement came into force on 2 January 1955 but by that date the trolleybuses were already history.

The first routes to succumb were those to Thorpe Bay via Bankside and the Kursaal and the branch to the Pier Head; there is some uncertainty as to when these routes last

In 1939 Southend Corporation acquired a batch of six AEC 661Ts – Nos 124-29 – that were fitted with Strachan bodywork. These were purchased as a result of the Southend-on-Sea Trolley Vehicles Order of 1939, which empowered the council to operate trolleybuses over the surviving tram routes. A further thirty-six vehicles were also ordered but the outbreak of war meant that these were never delivered. Four of the 1939 batch – Nos 124-27 – were loaned to Bradford Corporation between September 1940 and February 1942; Southend's livery of pale blue was to influence the decision of Bradford to change its livery from dark to a paler blue. The batch survived until the final closure of the Southend system in October 1954 with No 128 being the official last trolleybus. Here No 124 is seen on Eastwood Boulevard on 12 September 1954. *Gerald Druce/Online Transport Archive*

operated but, given the fact that they were summer only, some point during the autumn of 1953 would seem likely. This left the two circular routes – which had been connected as a cross-town service in 1951 – plus the route to the Kursaal via Southchurch Avenue operational.

These were to be converted in three stages. On 10 February 1954, the eastern circular was converted to motorbus operation; this was followed on 14 July 1954 by the conversion of the Kursaal route. Finally, on 28 October 1954, the western circular was converted. Of the trolleybuses, which had been housed in the corporation's London Road depot throughout their career, nine were sold to Doncaster – these were the Utility-bodied Sunbeam Ws delivered during 1945 and 1946 that were the last new trolleybuses purchased (fourteen second-hand vehicles were acquired in 1946 and 1950) – and the remainder were scrapped. No Southend trolleybus survives in preservation.

The last wholly new trolleybuses acquired by Southend were nine Sunbeam Ws that were new during 1945 and 1946. These were fitted with Utility bodies supplied by Brush (No 130) or Park Royal (Nos 131-38). The first of the Park Royal-bodied examples – No 131 – is pictured here. All nine of the Sunbeams were sold to Doncaster Corporation in 1954; they re-entered service as Nos 384-92 and were to be rebodied between 1956 and 1959. All were withdrawn finally between 1961 and 1963. *Harry Luff/ Online Transport Archive*

One of the six Park Royal-bodied Sunbeam Ws delivered during 1946 – No 135 – is pictured on the west circular service – route 28B – that operated anti-clockwise via Victoria Avenue, Fairfax Drive and London Road; this was destined to be Southend's final trolleybus route, being converted on 28 October 1954. By that date, however, all of the Utility-bodied Sunbeams had been withdrawn, all being taken out of service during 1953. *J. Joyce Collection/Online Transport Archive*

After the Second World War, Southend supplemented its fleet through the acquisition of second-hand vehicles; the first to be acquired were five single-deck Leyland TB3s – Nos 139-43 – that entered service in 1946. The quintet, fitted with Massey bodywork, had originally been delivered to the Teesside Railless Traction Board as Nos 9-13 in 1936; all five remained in service until 1952. No 141 is pictured at Southend Victoria station on 9 September 1950. *Julian Thompson/ Online Transport Archive*

The second source of second-hand trolleybuses to Southend Corporation was Wolverhampton Corporation, with nine pre-war Sunbeam MF2s making their way to Essex in 1950. No 152 – the highest numbered Southend trolleybus – was used on a Southern Counties Touring Society tour of the system on 17 September 1950; this had originally been Wolverhampton No 275 and like all of the ex-Wolverhampton vehicles was fitted with a Park Royal body. All nine remained in service until 1953. *John Meredith/Online Transport Archive*

Fleet number	Registration	Chassis	Body	New	Withdrawn	Notes
1 and 2; renumbered 101 and 102 in 1927	HJ5065/5389	Railless	Short	1925/26	1933	Hired originally and purchased 1927
103	NW9583	AEC 603T	Strachan & Brown B30F	1925	1937	Ex-demonstrator; acquired 1927
104	HJ7363	Garrett OS	Garrett H55RO	1927	1939	Ex-demonstrator; acquired 1928; displayed at 1927 Commercial Motor Show
105-09	HJ8925-8929	Garrett OS	Garrett H60R	1929	1939	
110 and 111	JN60/61	EE	EE H56D	1930	1939	Rebuilt as H56R 1937; sold to Nottingham
112-15	JN2112-2115	AEC 661T	EE L48R	1932	1950-54	Built with dummy radiators; 113/14 rebuilt 1948 without them
116	JN2086	AEC 663T	EE H55D (later H56R with front staircase removed)	1930	1950	Displayed at 1931 Commercial Motor Show; ex-demonstrator; acquired 1932; rebuilt
117-21	JN2817-2821	AEC661T	EE L48R	1933	1950-54	Built with dummy radiators; rebuilt without them in 1945
122	JN3822	GRCW	GRCW H54C	1933	1950	Displayed at 1933 Commercial Motor Show; on hire from November 1933; purchased 1934
123	JN4373	AEC Q	EE L56F	1934	1949	On hire from 1934; purchased 1935. Rebodied 1943 and 1945.
124-29	BHJ194-199	AEC 661T	Strachan H56R	1939	1954	
130	BHJ827	Sunbeam W	Brush UH56R	1945	1953	Sold to Doncaster Corporation as No 384
131-32	BHJ828-829	Sunbeam W	PR UH56R	1945	1953	Sold to Doncaster Corporation as Nos 385 and 386
133-38	BHJ898-903	Sunbeam W	PR UH56R	1946	1953	Sold to Doncaster Corporation as Nos 387-92

Fleet number	Registration	Chassis	Body	New	Withdrawn	Notes
139-43	VN9434-9438	Leyland TB3	Massey B32R	1936	1952	Ex-TRTB 9-13; acquired 1946
144-52	BDA364-69/ BJW171/173/175	Sunbeam MF2	PR H54R	1937/38	1953-54	Ex-Wolverhampton 264-69/71/73/75; acquired 1950

Route number	From	To	Date Opened	Date Closed	Notes
28A/28B	Victoria Circus	Prittlewell	16 October 1925	28 October 1954	Later part of Western circular service; 28A operated clockwork and 28B anti-clockwise
28C	Prittlewell	Priory Park	Whitsun 1926	28 October 1954	28C was workmen's service linking Priory Park terminus to Kursaal; route ceased operating autumn 1953
28A/28B	Priory Park	Eastwood Boulevard (via Fairfax Drive and Cavendish Gardens)	21 January 1932	28 October 1954	Later part of Western circular service; 28A operated clockwork and 28B anti-clockwise
52	High Street	Bankside	12 December 1928	Autumn 1953	
52	Bankside	Kursaal	2 August 1929	Autumn 1953	
	Marine Parade	Pier Head	21 June 1934	Autumn 1953	Service suspended during the Second World War
28	Eastwood Boulevard	Wellington Avenue (via Nelson Road)-Chalkwell Hall Schools	24 July 1935	28 October 1954	
51A	Kursaal	Thorpe Bay	4 June 1939	Autumn 1953	Service suspended during the Second World War; summer only service
28A/28B	Wellington Avenue – Chalkwell Hall Schools	Victoria Circus (via Nelson Road and London Road)	8 April 1942	28 October 1954	Western circular service; 28A operated clockwork and 28B anti-clockwise

Route number	From	To	Date Opened	Date Closed	Notes
51	Town Centre	Kursaal (via Southchurch Avenue)	8 April 1942	14 July 1954	
63A/63B	Town Centre (Bradley Street)	Hamstel Road (via Milton Street and North Avenue)	31 July 1932	10 February 1954	Later part of Eastern circular service; 63A operated clockwork and 63B anti-clockwise
63A/63B	Warrior Square	Bradley Street	1 June 1943	10 February 1954	
63/63A/63B	Southchurch Road (junction with Southchurch Avenue)	Southchurch	3 April 1944	10 February 1954	Eastern circular service; 63A operated clockwork and 63B anti-clockwise
63A/63B	Southchurch	Hamstel Road	3 April 1944	10 February 1954	Eastern circular service; 63A operated clockwork and 63B anti-clockwise
	North Avenue	Lonsdale Road	1945	10 February 1954	Short working for services along North Avenue

Service numbers (used from circa 1949)	Route
28	Town centre to Chalkwell Schools (Wellington Avenue)
28A	Western circular clockwise outbound via London Road
28B	Western circular anti-clockwise outbound via Victoria Avenue
28C	Priory Park to Kursaal (workmen's service)
51	Town centre via Southchurch Avenue to Kursaal
51A	Town centre via Southchurch Avenue and Kursaal to Thorpe Bay (summer only)
52	Town centre via Seaway and Marine Parade to Kursaal
52A	Town centre via Seaway and Kursaal to Thorpe Bay (summer only)
63	Warrior Square to Southchurch
63A	Eastern circular clockwise outbound via North Avenue
63B	Eastern circular anti-clockwise outbound via Southchurch Road

BIBLIOGRAPHY

Barker, Colin, et al; *Trolleybus Classics* series; Middleton Press; 1995 onwards

Blacker, Ken; *The London Trolleybus – Volume 1: 1931-1945*; Capital Transport; 2002

Bowen, D.G., and Callow, J.; *The Cardiff Trolleybus*; NTA; 1970

Buses Illustrated/Buses; Ian Allan Ltd; since 1949

Canneaux, T.P, and Hanson, N.H.; *The Trolleybuses of Newcastle upon Tyne 1936-1966 (Second Edition)*; Newcastle upon Tyne City Libraries; 1985

Challoner, Eric; *Trolleybus Days in Wolverhampton*; LRTA / Trolleybooks; 2017

Griffiths, Geoff; *Llanelly Trolleybuses*; Trolleybooks; 1992

Hall, D.A.; *Reading Trolleybuses*; Trolleybooks; 1991

Joyce, J., King, J. S. and Newman, A.G.; *British Trolleybus Systems*; Ian Allan Ltd; 1986

Joyce, J.; *Trolleybus Trails*; Ian Allan Ltd; 1963

King, J.S.; *Keighley Corporation Transport*; Advertiser Press; 1964

Kraemer-John, Glyn, and Bishop, John; *Trolleybus Memories: Brighton*; Ian Allan Publishing; 2007

Kraemer-Johnson, Glyn, and Bishop, John; *Trolleybus Memories: Brighton*; Ian Allan Publishing; 2007

Lockwood, Stephen; A-Z of British Trolleybuses; The Crowood Press; 2017

Lumb, Geoff; *Ian Allan Transport Library: British Trolleybuses 1911-1972*; Ian Allan Ltd; 1995

Mayou, Archie, Barker, Terry, and Stanford, John; *Birmingham Corporation Tramways: Trams and Trolleybuses*; Transport Publishing Co; 1982

Neale, R.F.A. (Ed); *London's Trolleybuses: A Fleet History*; PSV Circle / Omnibus Society; undated

Owen, Nicholas; *History of the British Trolleybus*; David & Charles; 1974

Potter, D. F., Webb, J. S. and Wilson, Ray; *Walsall Corporation Transport*; Birmingham Transport Historical Group; 1981

Scotney, D.J.S.; *The Maidstone Trolleybus*; NTA; 1972

Symons, R.D.H., and Creswell, P.R.; *British Trolleybuses*; Ian Allan Ltd; 1967

Taylor, Hugh; *London Trolleybus Routes*; Capital Transport; 1994

Taylor, Hugh; *London Trolleybuses: A Class Album*; Capital Transport; 2006

Trolleybus Magazine; National Trolleybus Association

Turner, Keith, Smith, Paul and Smith, Shirley; *The Directory of British Tram Depots*; OPC; 2001

Walsall's Trolleybuses; West Midlands PTE; 1970

Webber, Mick; *London Trolleybus Chronology*; Ian Allan Publishing; 1997